The Collector's Encyclopedia of

COOKIE JARS

Fred Roerig
and
Joyce Herndon Roerig

COLLECTOR BOOKS
A Division of Schroeder Publishing Co., Inc.

The current values in this book should be used only as a guide. They are not intended to set prices, which vary from one section of the country to another. Auction prices as well as dealer prices vary greatly and are affected by condition as well as demand. Neither the Authors nor the Publisher assumes responsibility for any losses that might be incurred as a result of consulting this guide.

Additional copies of this book may be ordered from:

Collector Books
P.O. Box 3009
Paducah, KY 42002-3009

or

Fred & Joyce Roerig
Route 2, Box 504
Walterboro, SC 29488

@$24.95. Add $2.00 for postage and handling.

Dedication

This book is dedicated in loving memory to W.H. (Bill) Herndon Sr., the father of Joyce, our very special friend.

This Herndon, of Scottish descent, was entirely too practical to have "waded" right into this collection, but he would have eventually come around. And, with a twinkle in his eyes, either he would have brought us a cookie jar or told us where to look.

Joyce's father never knew of our collection, or our book. He died at the age of fifty-two. Maybe, in some way, this will include him.

Acknowledgments

First and foremost, thanks to Charles and Rose Snyder who packed and hauled box after box of jars of their collection from Kansas to Missouri; Rena London who unselfishly shared all of her records and encouragement; Edna Myers, Leslie Wolfe, and Lois Lehner who contributed personal correspondence, old company catalog sheets, magazine clippings, etc.; Judy Posner, Jeff Mazur, Stephanie Neuman, Paul Jeromack, and Roger Mraz who all took photos of special jars in their own collections to contribute; Juarine Wooldridge, Don and Katherine Braly, Bob and Betty Perry, Leonard Rothstein, Mrs. R.A. Allen, Carolyn Roscoe, and Tom Davis, who all loaned us items for photography; Frank Lewin of Marshall Field, Jack and Carol Jessen, Ruth Kleeman, Bunny Walker, Debbie Rees, Johnnie Dixon, who were always ready to answer questions and offer encouragement; Mr. and Mrs. Charles Allen of American Bisque, Don Winton of Twin Winton, and Harold Roman of California Originals, Roman Ceramics, and Cumberland Ware who gave invaluable assistance; Melva Davern and Jo Cunningham who pushed and pushed; Paula Herndon Polk who flunked Joyce in grammar, but being a "southern lady," she was too polite to admit it. A special thank-you to our only son, Bill Roerig, who has been a mainstay in every way in helping to complete this book.

To the collectors everywhere who have been patiently waiting goes our gratitude.

Thanks, Tom Davis, commercial photographer of Springfield, Missouri, for the wonderful photography and sense of humor which almost made the chaos fun. Also, our appreciation to Curtis & Mays Studio in Paducah, Kentucky, for the final additions we felt we needed to add.

Last, but certainly not least, thank you, Bill Schroeder, for giving us the opportunity to fulfill a dream.

Introduction

I have always loved cookie jars, picking them up as they struck my fancy, never thinking of them as a collection. As a family, we have been collecting cookie jars for many years. The Roerig children are all brainwashed. They think cookie jar collecting is the norm and they can spot a great cookie jar a mile away.

Cookie jar collecting is an adventure. Being dairy farmers, plus working at outside jobs, most of our excursions in the beginning were between milkings and on the weekends. When we heard from a collector friend about an upcoming cookie jar auction in Indiana, which was to include *Dino*, we felt we had to attend. The auction could not compare to Andy Warhol's, but it surely seemed like it at the time. There were two buyers present; both were determined to own that *Dino*. Well, *Dino* was bound for Missouri no matter which bidder was the victor. I am glad we were not after the gold-trimmed Shawnee *Pig Bank/Cookie Jar* or the fantastically mint McCoy *Indian.* We might have had to hitchhike home carrying *Dino.*

Another time, a Texas dealer from Canton took me to a booth to see a jar he could not decide about its being authentic or worth the price. Lo and behold, it was the Pearl China *Watermelon Mammy.* There I stood, discreetly poking the owner of the jar, trying to signal to him that I wanted it, but to no avail. Finally, unable to contain myself one minute longer, I said, "If you're not going to buy that jar, I am." The tactic worked; I own the jar.

One weekend we crossed the Arkansas line, just wandering. We came across a shop, but we found nothing. The shop owner offered to open the adjacent shop which belonged to his brother and which had a few cookie jars. Sitting on the shelf was *Olive Oyl.* I was so excited but Fred would not buy it and leave. He kept saying, "Wait a minute." I thought the man had lost his mind. However, Fred's eye was a lot better than mine, because sitting practically next to *Olive Oyl* was the single *Joe Carioca,* which I would have missed.

Collecting is also stressful. Can you imagine standing in a booth with half a gold-trimmed Brush *Davy Crockett* and another dealer is holding the other half? It happens.

Many cookie jar collectors are also curious about the dates of production and companies which produced them; so when any type of dating was available through old catalog sheets or other sources, we have supplied it. Otherwise, we have tried to supply the dates the companies were actually in business and/or producing cookie jars. The pottery companies remind me of living in a small town where everyone is related to everyone else, but sometimes the puzzle is unworkable. These companies were so plagued with floods and fires that it is a miracle any information at all can be retrieved. We sincerely hope this book is helpful.

Enjoy collecting. We have made many lifetime friends and have never had a problem striking up conversation with collectors.

--- Joyce Roerig

Hints to Collectors

Buy what you like. We have seen cookie jar "want" lists from people with jars listed we did not even know. When asked about these jars, the individual did not know what the jar was and had only seen it on another list. Personally, we hate lists. We have always been afraid we would miss something great, simply because we did not know it existed and therefore had omitted it from the list.

Do not hesitate to buy a new jar if you like it. We are so glad we purchased the McCoy *Baseball Boy* and *Football Boy* for our son when they were issued; the jars are mint and were affordable. Cookie jars are not released to every part of the country, so some will slip by you. It is really hard to predict what will "click," so again, buy only what you truly like.

Neither the age nor the manufacturer determine collectibility. Vandor's *Betty Boop* is a great example of this. "Black" and "Character" jars seem destined to grow in popularity. Who would have dreamed the *Little Black Girl* in the *Sears Catalog* a few years ago would be where she is today. Joyce's twin sisters were smart enough to buy her; ours was a little harder to acquire.

We have been asked many times about retouching and repainting jars. Our opinion is that skillful painting in the original colors will not subtract from the value. Alas, "skillful" and "original" are the key words here and can cause problems.

Beware of reproductions. A duplicate is usually made by making a mold from the original product. These items will be smaller and, invariably, of lesser quality weightwise than the original. If you know you are buying a reproduction and want a shelf piece, in expectation of purchasing the original, or if you just like the new product, proceed with the purchase. We do not consider the new Vandor *Howdy Doody* to be a reproduction because it is not from the original mold. It is a nice jar and probably will become very collectible.

Know your dealers. Very few people are able to comb the entire country and therefore need some assistance. We think many of the established dealers have as much fun searching for jars for their customers as the customers themselves do. Reliable dealers are essential to a collector.

In summary, remember to buy what you like, consider the newer releases, make your own decisions about retouching or repainting, beware of reproductions, and know your dealers. Most of all, ENJOY!

Abingdon

"The clear ring of fine china"

The Abingdon Pottery Company of Abingdon, Illinois, started production in 1934 but did not produce its first cookie jar until 1939. A total of twenty-two designs were manufactured before the Abingdon artware era ended in 1950.

With rare exception, Abingdon jars have an ink stamp, "Abingdon USA," plus an impressed serial number. We have never seen a true Abingdon cookie jar without the serial number.

All colors were fired; no "cold" paint (paint that washes off) was used.

The dates shown indicate the start of production.

ROW 1: *Daisy* (1949), "Abingdon USA, 677." Accessories are available for the *Daisy* jar, but are not pictured. There is a matching range set consisting of salt and pepper shakers and a drippings jar, plus a tea set with teapot, cream pitcher, and sugar bowl. $38.00-42.00

Three Bears, "Abingdon USA, 696" $50.00-55.00

Little Girl, "Abingdon USA, 693" $48.00-52.00

ROW 2: *Mother Goose,* "Abingdon USA, 695" $175.00-185.00

Miss Muffet, "Abingdon USA, 622" (1949) $115.00-120.00

Bo Peep, "694." The *Little Bo Peep* pictured is not an Abingdon. It has the right serial number but not the ink stamp. The correct colors are shown in the original catalog sheets to follow. The price reflects the actual Abingdon *Bo Peep*. This copy is slightly less. $130.00-140.00

ROW 3: *Pineapple*, "Abingdon USA, 664" (1949) $48.00-52.00

Hippo, "Abingdon USA, 549" decoration "C" (1942). In 1942, Abingdon introduced colorful hand-painted decorations, which greatly added to the appeal of "Oswald," the hippo. $185.00-190.00

Pumpkin, "674" (1949). This delightful jack o' lantern is not an Abingdon for it lacks the ink stamp, but it is from the Abingdon mold, complete with serial number. The color tones are much more vivid than the original Abingdon. The price reflects the Abingdon *Pumpkin*. $140.00-150.00

"COOKY"

The first cookie jar Abingdon produced in 1939 was the *Little Old Lady* in solid colors.

ROW 1:	*Little Old Lady*, "471." Only the number is visible on this jar, due to the color.	$85.00-95.00
	Little Old Lady, "Abingdon USA 471." Decoration "B" (1942)	$90.00-100.00
	Little Old Lady, "Abingdon USA 471" (1939)	$65.00-75.00
ROW 2:	*Choo Choo,* "Abingdon USA 651" (1949)	$68.00-72.00
	Jack-in-the-Box, "Abingdon USA 611" (1947)	$125.00-135.00
	Hobby Horse, "Abingdon USA 602" (1947)	$90.00-100.00
ROW 3:	*Clock,* "Abingdon USA 653" (1949)	$50.00-60.00
	Humpty Dumpty, "Abingdon USA 663" (1949)	$115.00-125.00
	Money Bag, "Abingdon USA 588" (1947)	$48.00-52.00
BELOW:	*Wigwam,* "Abingdon USA 665" (1949)	$195.00-205.00
	Baby, "Abingdon USA 561"	$110.00-120.00
	Witch, "Abingdon USA 692"	$150.00-160.00

COOKIES
COOKIE TIME
$ COOKIES

ROW 1:	*Windmill*, "Abingdon USA, 678" (1949)	$90.00-100.00
	Fat Boy, "Abingdon USA, 495" (1941)	$80.00-90.00
	Choo Choo, "Abingdon USA, 651" (1941)	$68.00-72.00
ROW 2:	*Little Old Lady*, "Abingdon USA, 471" Decoration "A" (1942)	$90.00-100.00
	Little Old Lady, "Abingdon USA, 471" (1939)	$65.00-70.00
	Little Old Lady, "Abingdon USA, 471" Decoration "C" (1942)	$185.00-195.00
ROW 3:	*Hippo*, "Abingdon USA, 549" (1941)	$80.00-90.00
	Hippo, "Abingdon USA, 549" (1941)	$80.00-90.00
	Hippo, "Abingdon USA, 549" (1941)	$80.00-90.00

Pages 12 and 13 show 1950 catalog sheets from Abingdon.

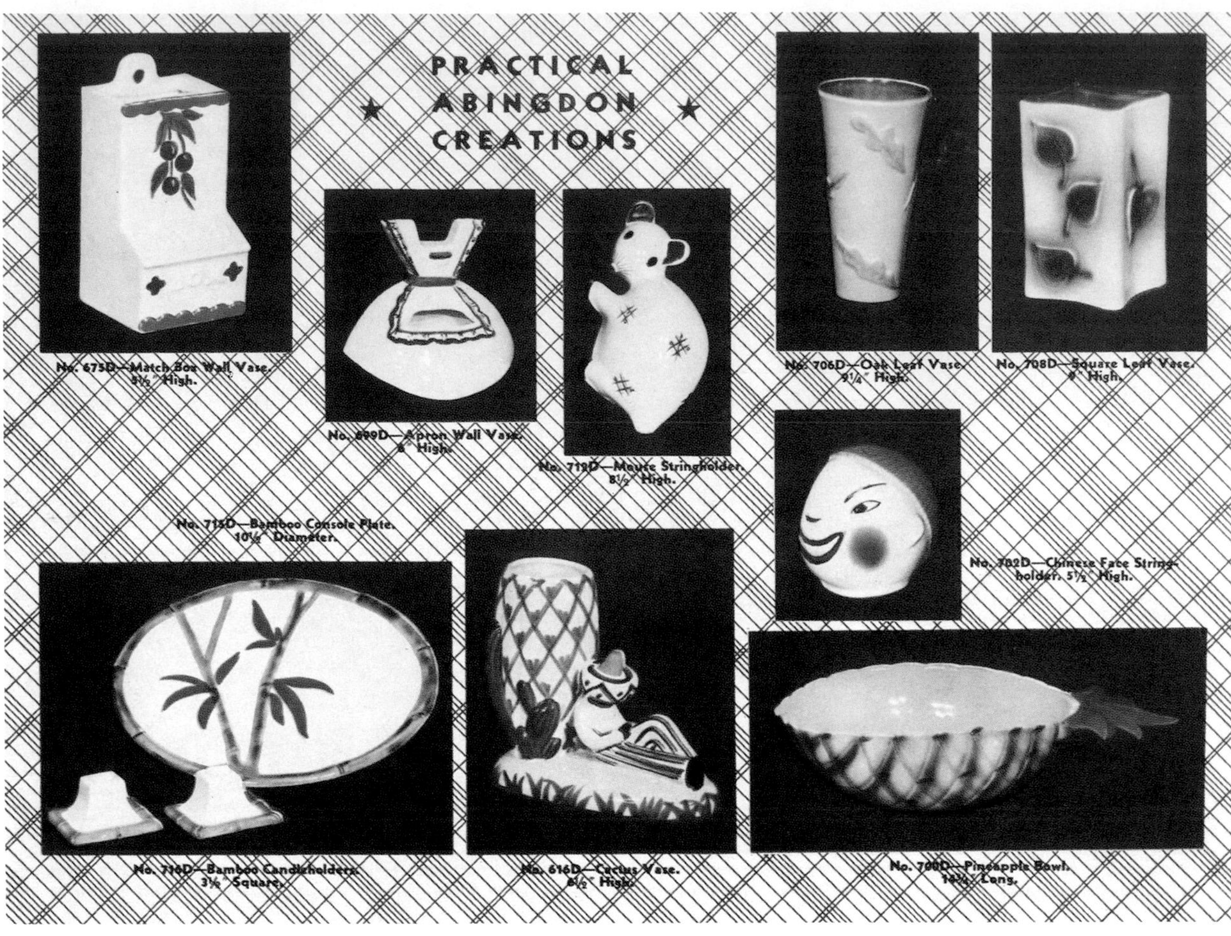

PRACTICAL ★ ABINGDON ★ CREATIONS

No. 675D—Match Box Wall Vase. 5½" High.

No. 699D—Apron Wall Vase. 8" High.

No. 712D—Mouse Stringholder. 8½" High.

No. 706D—Oak Leaf Vase. 9¼" High.

No. 708D—Square Leaf Vase. 9" High.

No. 715D—Bamboo Console Plate. 10½" Diameter.

No. 702D—Chinese Face Stringholder. 5½" High.

No. 716D—Bamboo Candleholders. 3½" Square.

No. 616D—Cactus Vase. 6½" High.

No. 700D—Pineapple Bowl. 14¾" Long.

No. 663D—Humpty Dumpty Cookie Jar. 10½" High.

No. 662D—Miss Muffet Cookie Jar. 11" High.

No. 677D—Daisy Cookie Jar. 8" High. Individually Packed in Mailable Carton. (See Page 7.)

No. 697DF—Floral Cookie Jar. 8½" High. Individually Packed in Mailable Carton.

No. 696D—Three Bears Cookie Jar. 8¾" High.

No. 697DP—Plaid Cookie Jar. 8½" High.

No. 693D—Little Girl Cookie Jar. 9½" High.

No. 653D—Clock Cookie Jar. 9" High.

ABINGDON
ART POTTERY

No. 677D
Daisy Cookie Jar
8" High

You may select this particular Cookie Jar in either of the two color combinations shown on this page. Specify your preference when ordering.

This Cookie Jar only is individually packed in a mailable carton.

No. 690D
Daisy Range Set

Each Range Set consists of 1 Drippings Jar 4½" High and 1 Salt and Pepper Set 4" High.

Range Set may be ordered in your choice of two different color combinations as shown on this page. Specify whether Blue or Yellow decoration is desired.

Each Daisy Range Set is packed complete in an individual mailable carton.

No. 666D
Jam Set with 8" Tray

No. 666J
3 Jam Jars Only
3½" High

This attractive Jam Set has Jars in Jonquil Yellow. The Lids are in Ivory. Each Lid is decorated with an individual kind of fruit; a plum, a strawberry, grapes. Tray is in Ivory banded in Green. Set of Jam Jars may be purchased with or without Tray. Each set packed in mailable carton.

No. 691D
Daisy Tea Set

Each Tea Set consists of 1 Tea Pot 6¼" High, 1 Cream Pitcher 2½" High, and 1 Sugar Bowl 3" High.

Tea Set may be ordered in your choice of the two color combinations shown on this page. Specify preference.

Tea Set is individually packed in mailable carton.

No. 695D—Mother Goose Cookie Jar.
12" High.

No. 588D—Money Bag Cookie Jar.
7½" High.

No. 664D—Pineapple Cookie Jar.
10½" High.

No. 651D—Choo Choo Cookie Jar.
7½" High.

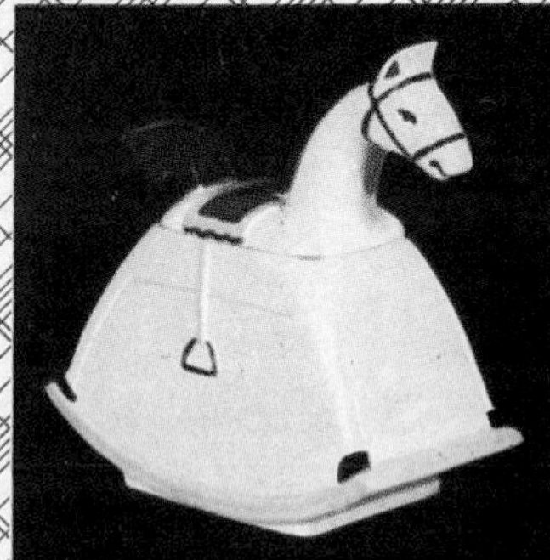

No. 602D—Hobby Horse Cookie Jar.
10½" High.

No. 674D—Pumpkin Cookie Jar.
8" High.

No. 694D—Bo Peep Cookie Jar.
12" High.

No. 692D—Witch Cookie Jar.
11½" High.

PAGE 8

Advertisement

What an excellent medium for a company to use to present its product to the public, especially the cookie jar collecting public.

ROW 1: *Keebler Tree House*, unmarked. This jar was originally produced for Keebler by the Haeger Pottery Company and was available directly from Keebler with a coupon and proof of purchase. $50.00-55.00

Ernie, the Keebler Elf, "F&F Mold & Die Works, Dayton, Ohio" $48.00-52.00

Ernie, matching mug, "F&F Mold and Die Works, Dayton, Ohio" $10.00-15.00

Frango Mint Chip Cookies, Marshall Field and Company, unmarked. The original jar box states "Made in Italy." Frango Mint is a registered trademark for Field's Frango Mints. $38.00-42.00

ROW 2: *Nabisco,* "McCoy 78, Lancaster Colony, USA," made in 1974. McCoy also made a 4 foot-high model of this jar to kick off the promotional tour for Nabisco. $50.00-55.00

Barnum's Animal Crackers, "152, USA." This jar was produced by McCoy in 1972 and 1973. $100.00-125.00

Frango Mint Truck, "Made in Italy Expressly for Marshall Field and Company." $38.00-42.00

ROW 3: *Nestle Toll House Cookies,* unmarked, recipe on back, believed to be produced by Holiday Designs. $60.00-65.00

Ken-L-Ration Dog, "F&F Mold and Die Works, Dayton, Ohio" $48.00-52.00

Cat and Dog salt and pepper, "F&F Mold and Die Works, Dayton, Ohio" $12.00-15.00

Avon Bear, unmarked. This cookie jar was made for Avon by California Originals in 1979. It was originally presented as a promotional gift to Avon teamleaders. $40.00-45.00

Keebler
Marshall Field's Company
frango mint
chip cookies

NABISCO
NABISCO
BARNUM'S ANIMALS
CRACKERS

Original
TOLL HOUSE
Cookies

ROW 1: *"Aramis Bear"* $30.00-40.00

Kraft-T-Bear, "Genuine Regal China, made in USA, Kraft Inc.," personalized with T-Bear paw print and signature impressed. $100.00-115.00

Bear, "148 USA," referred to as the *Hamm's Bear,* made by McCoy. $80.00-85.00

ROW 2: *Quaker Oats,* "Regal China," below recipe on the back. $85.00-95.00

Jim Beam Jar, Bottle Club membership gift for the year 1975-76, featuring the logo "The International Association of Jim Beam Bottles & Specialties Clubs." $45.00-50.00

Gold Medal Cookies, tin

Pillsbury Doughboy, "The Pillsbury Co. 1973." The original *Pillsbury Doughboy* mold, owned by California Originals, was sold to Holiday Designs, and re-issued, complete with the 1973 date. It is impossible to distinguish between the two productions. $35.00-40.00

Pillsbury Doughboy salt and pepper, unmarked $8.00-10.00

ROW 3: *Elsie* cookie jar, unmarked Pottery Guild $85.00-95.00

Elsie Bust combination salt and pepper, "(C) The Borden Co." $18.00-22.00

Elmer and Elsie salt and pepper, unmarked $22.00-25.00

Elmer and Elsie cream and sugar, unmarked $40.00-50.00

Elsie Lamp, unmarked $50.00-60.00

Elsie and Beauregard mugs, "Universal-Cambridge" $20.00-25.00

Elmer and Elsie sugar and cream, unmarked $40.00-50.00

I Love
MARSHMALLOWS

OLD FASHIONED
QUAKER
OATS
INTERNATIONAL ASSOCIATION OF
JIM BEAM BOTTLE & SPECIALTIES CLUBS
Gold
MEDAL
Cookies
COOKIES

Elsie
Elmer
BEAUREGARD
ELSIE

ROW 1: *Famous Amos,* "Treasure Craft copyright, Made in USA" $28.00-32.00

Keebler Cookies and Milk, "Louisiana Plastics Inc., St. Louis, Missouri." The jar comes complete with four tumblers. $12.00-15.00

Keebler Tree House, "350 USA," manufactured by McCoy (1986-1987) $35.00-40.00

Grandma's Cookies, paper label, "Made in USA by Kromex." Grandma's Brand is a registered trademark of Frito Lay. $20.00-25.00

ROW 2: *Coke Jug,* "1004 USA," produced by McCoy (1986 to present) $45.00-55.00

Coke Can, "1003 USA," Produced by McCoy (1986 to present) $45.00-55.00

Century 21 $80.00-90.00

ROW 3: *Sprout,* "Copyright 1988, The Pillsbury Company, Made in Taiwan" $35.00-45.00

Sprout salt and pepper, unmarked $8.00-10.00

Pound Puppy, "PP" in heart on the hip, sticker, "Pound Puppies Lovable, Huggable Exclusively Distributed by United Silver & Cutlery Co. copyright 1987 Tonka Corp. Made in Taiwan" $20.00-25.00

Almost Home, inside jar, "Almost-Home 1986 Limited Edition of 20,000." This cookie jar was produced by Holiday-Designs of Sebring, Ohio, which went out of business in 1986. $50.00-60.00

Famous Amos
Keebler
Grand Ma's
COOKIES
DELICIOUS
REFRESHING
Coca-Cola
Coke
Trade-mark
Century 21
REAL ESTATE
SOLD
AMERICA'S NUMBER 1 TOP SELLER, CENTURY 21

American Bisque

The American Bisque Company had its beginnings in Williamstown, West Virginia, in 1919. Cookie jars were produced from 1930 until 1973.

The company was an Allen family tradition. Though not originally started by the Allen family, it was owned by the family from 1922 until its sale in 1982.

B.E. Allen was the original Allen to own American Bisque. After selling his interest in the American Pottery Company of Marietta, Ohio, and buying the remainder of the stock in American Bisque, of which he was already part owner, Mr. Allen was joined by his son, A.N. Allen.

From A.N. Allen came Charles M. Allen. He was also a vital part of American Bisque management. When the Allen family sold out their interest, Charles remained until its closing in 1983.

We automatically think of wedges when we think of American Bisque, however, many of their early jars, recently identified by the Allen family, make us look more closely. Some of these jars are photographed in the Miscellaneous section.

ROW 1:	*Boy Pig,* unmarked	$35.00-45.00
	Lady Pig, unmarked (1958)	$35.00-45.00
	Pig with Straw Hat, "USA"	$40.00-50.00
ROW 2:	*Elephant with Ball Cap,* "USA"	$45.00-50.00
	Baby Elephant, unmarked	$48.00-52.00
	Sailor Elephant, "USA"	$45.00-50.00
ROW 3:	*Jack-in-Box,* "USA" (1958)	$35.00-38.00
	Dancing Elephant, unmarked	$48.00-52.00
	Umbrella Kids, "USA 739"	$70.00-80.00

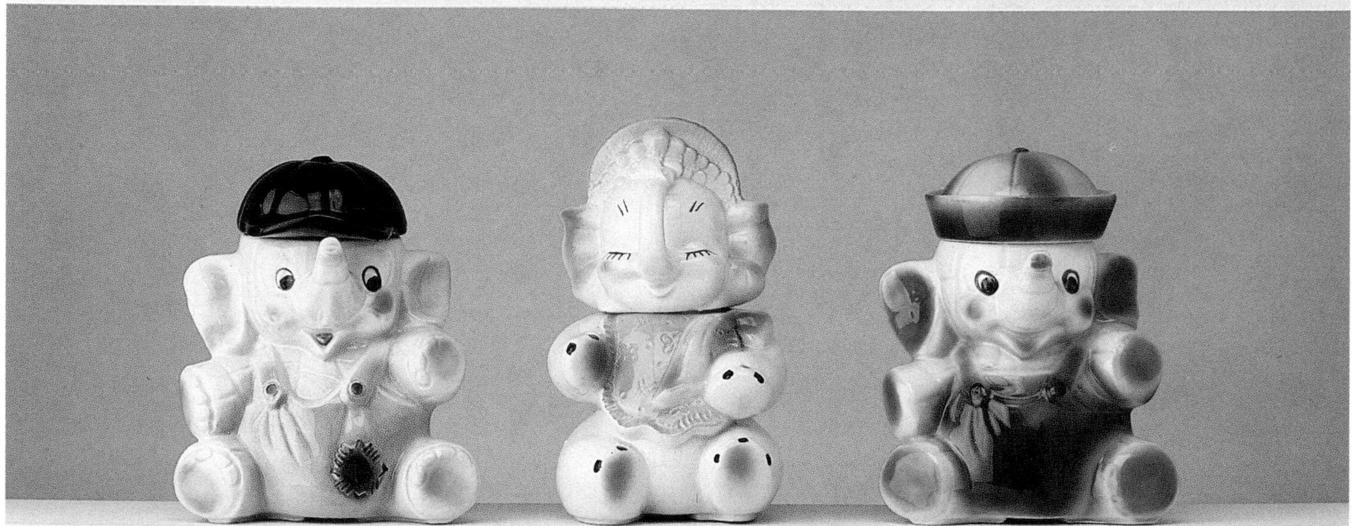

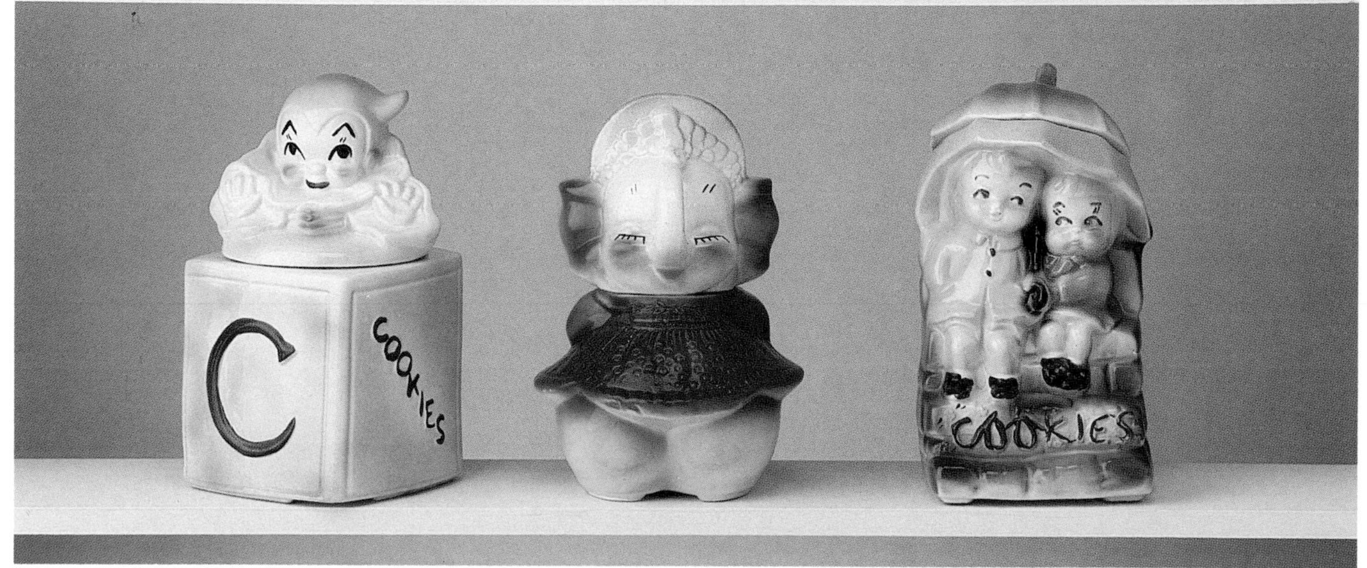
C
COOKIES
COOKIES

ROW 1:	*Cylinder with Bluebirds,* unmarked	$20.00-22.00
	Sack of Cookies, "USA"	$28.00-32.00
	Gift Box, "USA" (1958)	$45.00-50.00
ROW 2:	*Kitten & Beehive,* "USA" (1958)	$30.00-35.00
	Basket O'Cookies, "USA" (1958)	$28.00-32.00
	Puppy, "USA" (1958)	$35.00-38.00
ROW 3:	*Cookie Barrel,* "USA"	$12.00-15.00
	After School Cookies, "USA 741"	$25.00-30.00
	Cylinder with Daisies, "USA"	$20.00-22.00

Cookies
COOKIES
COOKIES
COOKIE BARREL
AFTER SCHOOL COOKIES

ROW 1:	*Kittens and Yarn,* "ABC" This larger version of the kittens and yarn is considered by many collectors to be Walt Disney's Figaro. Figaro was the model, but this particular cookie jar is not a licensed Disney product.	$40.00-50.00
	Rooster, "USA"	$38.00-42.00
	Carrousel, "USA"	$38.00-42.00
ROW 2:	*French Poodle,* "USA" (1959)	$42.00-45.00
	Tugboat, with bell in lid, "USA"	$85.00-95.00
	Little Girl Lamb, "USA"	$40.00-45.00
ROW 3:	*Majorette,* "USA"	$70.00-75.00
	Clown with Raised Arms, "USA"	$35.00-38.00
	Collegiate Owl, "USA" (1958)	$35.00-40.00

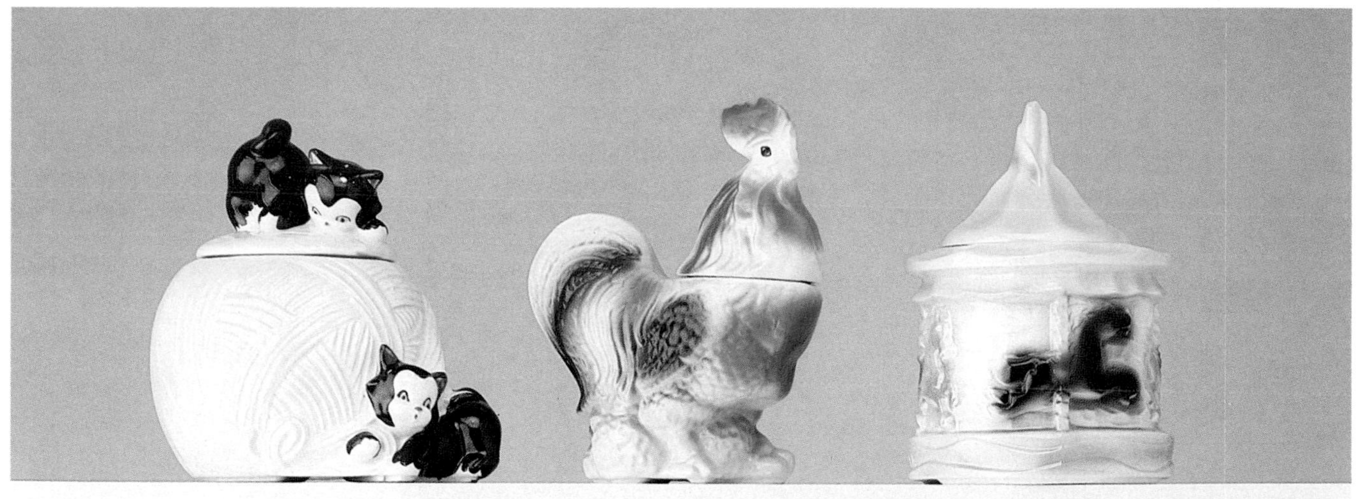

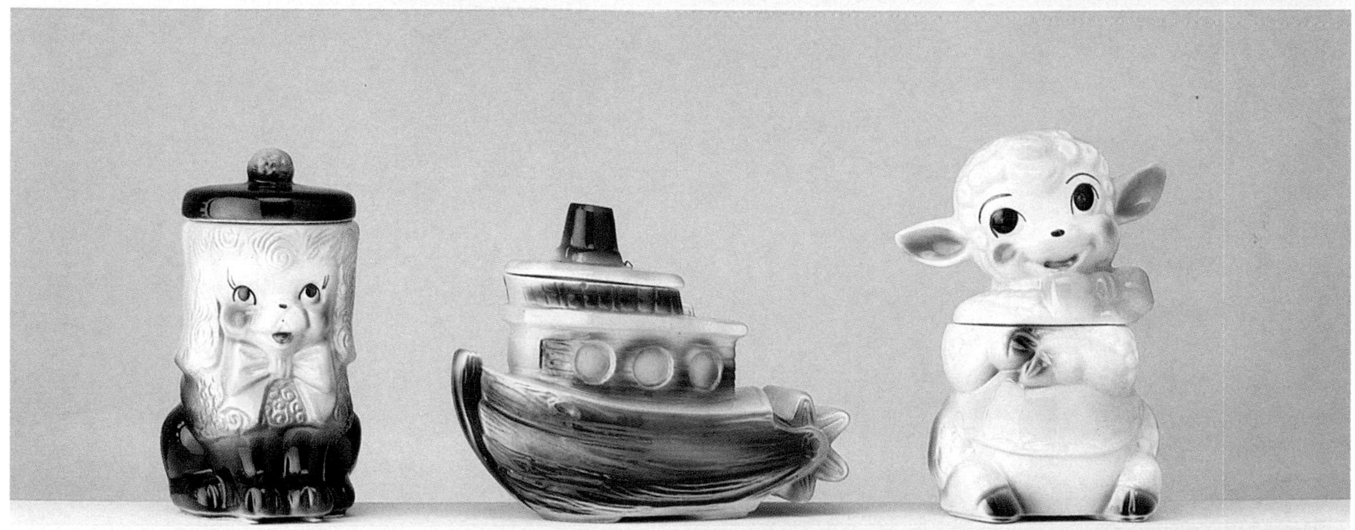

COOKIES

ROW1:	*Churn,* "USA" (1958)	$18.00-22.00
	Feed Bag, "USA" (1958)	$20.00-25.00
	Coffee Pot, "USA" (1958). The *Churn, Feed Bag,* and *Coffee Pot* series are also available with blue flowers and accessory pieces, such as salt and pepper shakers, grease jar, pitcher, and glasses.	$18.00-22.00
ROW 2:	*Boy Bear,* "USA"	$32.00-35.00
	Bear with hat , "USA"	$38.00-40.00
	Girl Bear, unmarked (1958)	$32.00-35.00
ROW 3:	*Engine,* "USA"	$38.00-42.00
	Cookies and Milk, "USA 740"	$65.00-70.00
	Cookie Truck, "USA"	$35.00-38.00

COOKIES
COOKIES
& MILK
COOKIE
TRUCK

This series of "Flashers" produced by American Bisque are really unique and sought after by the serious collector.

ROW 1:	*Tortoise and Hare,* "803 USA"	$90.00-95.00
	Cow Over Moon, "806 USA"	$95.00-98.00
	Bear with Honey, "Corner Cookie Jar, 804 USA"	$75.00-80.00
ROW 2:	*Kids Watching TV,* "801 Sandman Cookies"	$55.00-60.00
	Clown on Stage, "805 USA"	$50.00-55.00
	Cheerleaders, "Corner Cookie Jar, 802 USA"	$75.00-80.00
ROW 3:	*Grandma,* "USA" (1958)	$40.00-45.00
	Yarn Doll, unmarked	$50.00-55.00
	Dutch Girl, "USA" (1958)	$35.00-38.00

Below:	*Space Ship,* "USA"	$80.00-90.00
	Lamb with Flower, "USA"	$50.00-60.00
	Recipe Jar, unmarked	$40.00-50.00

COOKIES
HAVE A COOKIE

ROW 1:	*Ring Jar,* "USA"	$15.00-18.00
	Pedestal Jar, "USA"	$15.00-18.00
	Spool of Thread with thimble finial, "USA"	$30.00-35.00
ROW 2:	*Ring for Cookies,* bell in lid, "USA"	$28.00-32.00
	Pine Cone Coffee Pot, "USA"	$25.00-28.00
	Animal Crackers, "USA"	$15.00-18.00
ROW 3:	*School House,* bell in lid, "USA"	$28.00-32.00
	Apple Design Cylinder, "USA"	$15.00-18.00
	Tea Kettle, "USA," Martha and George Washington type figures. The Allen family does not remember ever producing this jar and does not feel that it looks like their work. It is truly difficult to identify every jar properly. Here we were basing our judgment on the wedges and quality.	$18.00-22.00

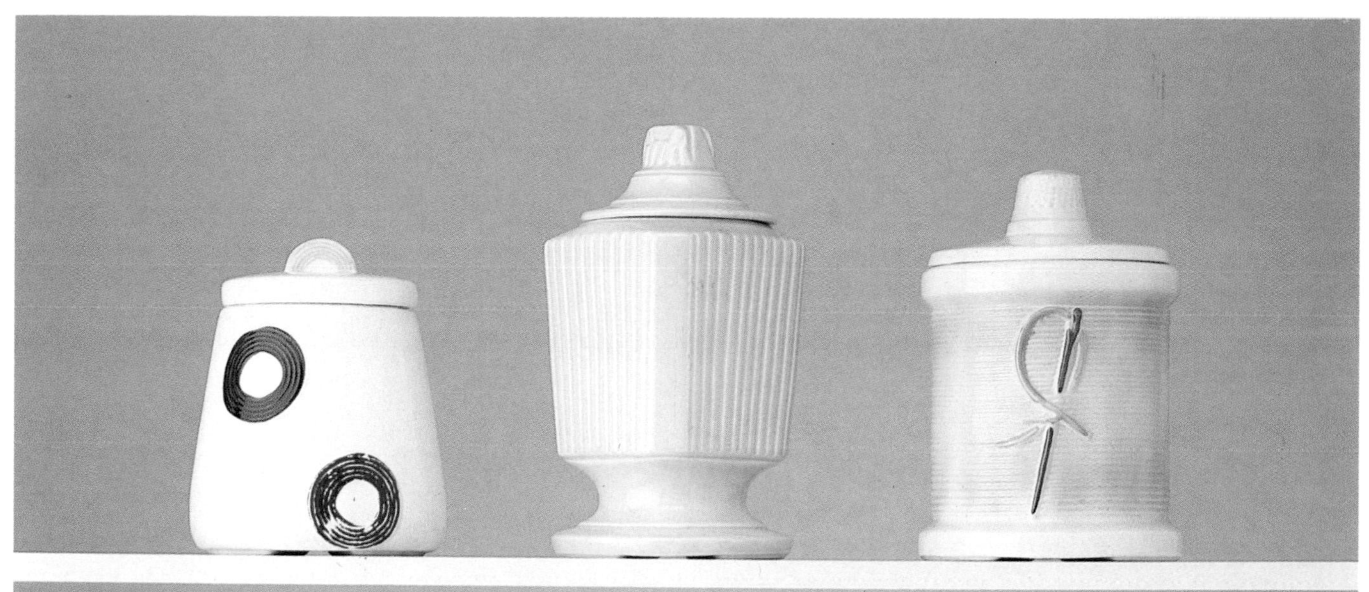

RING
FOR
COOKIES
COOKIES

AFTER SCHOOL
COOKIES

All of the jars shown on this page are a collector's delight and are highly sought after for their unique designs.

ROW 1:	*Blackboard Hobo,* "USA"	$80.00-85.00
	Blackboard Clown, "USA"	$70.00-75.00
	Blackboard Girl, "USA"	$80.00-85.00
ROW 2:	*Davy Crockett,* "USA"	$175.00-180.00
	Davy Crockett, "USA"	$165.00-175.00
	Blackboard Boy, "USA"	$80.00-85.00
ROW 3:	*Boots,* "USA 742"	$70.00-75.00
	Saddle Blackboard, "USA"	$85.00-90.00
	Horse, "USA." We had more difficulty finding the horse several years ago than any cookie jar on this page. We still have never seen another one for sale, although we know they have been found by other collectors.	$175.00-185.00

BELOW: *Mohawk Indian,* unmarked. This little Indian was modeled for the Mohawk Carpet Company. $185.00-195.00

MUSN'T FORGET
DON'T FORGET
REMEMBER!
DAVY CROCKETT
DAVY CROCKETT
DON'T FORGET
COOKIES
MUSN'T FORGET

ROW 1:	*Soldier,* "743 USA." See the Walt Disney section for another version of this jar.	$28.00-32.00
	Flower Jar, "USA"	$18.00-22.00
	Pot Belly Stove, "USA"	$18.00-22.00
ROW 2:	*SS Kookie,* "USA"	$42.00-48.00
	Sailor Elephant, "USA"	$40.00-45.00
	Chick, "USA" (1959)	$32.00-35.00
ROW 3:	*Clown,* "USA" (1959)	$32.00-35.00
	Carrousel, "USA"	$18.00-22.00
	Magic Bunny, "USA" (1959)	$32.00-35.00

SS KOOKIE
COOKIES

Here is another page showing some of the harder to find American Bisque jars. The little dutch couple wins the popularity contest at our house.

ROW 1: *Mr. Rabbit,* "USA" $50.00-55.00

Mrs. Rabbit, "USA" (1959) $50.00-55.00

Pig-in-Poke, "USA" (1958) $35.00-40.00

ROW 2: *Picnic Basket,* "USA." The lid is actually a tray for cookies. $75.00-80.00

Pennsylvania Dutch Girl, "USA" $120.00-130.00

Pennsylvania Dutch Boy, "USA" $120.00-130.00

ROW 3: *Seal on Igloo,* "USA" $68.00-72.00

Peasant Girl, "USA" $95.00-105.00

Treasure Chest, "USA" (1959) $50.00-55.00

BELOW: *Chef* with tray, "603 USA" $110.00-125.00

Grandma, unmarked. This is another example of ABC's gold trim. $85.00-95.00

Milk Can with bell in lid, "USA" $30.00-35.00

COOKIES

COOKIE TRAY

ROW 1:	*Dutch Boy,* "USA"	$35.00-38.00
	Rooster with heavy gold trim, unmarked	$68.00-72.00
	Bow Bear, "USA"	$35.00-38.00
ROW 2:	*Dog,* "USA" (1959). The little dog sits atop a quilted base.	$35.00-38.00
	Modern Rooster, "USA"	$35.00-38.00
	Kitten, "USA" (1959) The kitten sits atop a quilted base.	$35.00-38.00
ROW 3:	*Cookie Railroad,* "USA." Has three wedges, due to the length.	$35.00-38.00
	Kittens & Yarn "USA" (1959)	$28.00-32.00
	Elephant with gold trim, unmarked	$115.00-125.00

COOKIE R.R.

We call this series "Hands-in-the-Pockets" since all the bases are molded with their hands in their pockets, with the exception of the turnabout baby. American Bisque Company never produced a turnabout. The molds are so similar that the best way to identify is to look for the "USA."

ROW 1: *Mr. and Mrs. Pig Turnabout,* unmarked, APCO $55.00-65.00

Cat, not turnabout, "USA," ABC $48.00-52.00

Cow/Bull Turnabout, unmarked, APCO $55.00-65.00

ROW 2: *Rabbit,* miniature version, not turnabout but bank in lid, unmarked, ABC $48.00-52.00

Baby, happy/sad, boy/girl turnabout, unmarked, APCO $65.00-75.00

Bull, not turnabout, unmarked, ABC $48.00-52.00

ROW 3: *Rabbit,* lid has a great resemblance to "Thumper," "USA," ABC $48.00-52.00

Pig, single, not turnabout or bank, "USA," ABC $48.00-52.00

Elephant, combination, bank in lid, "USA," ABC $48.00-52.00

BELOW: A second version of the happy/sad, boy/girl *Baby,* unmarked, APCO $65.00-75.00

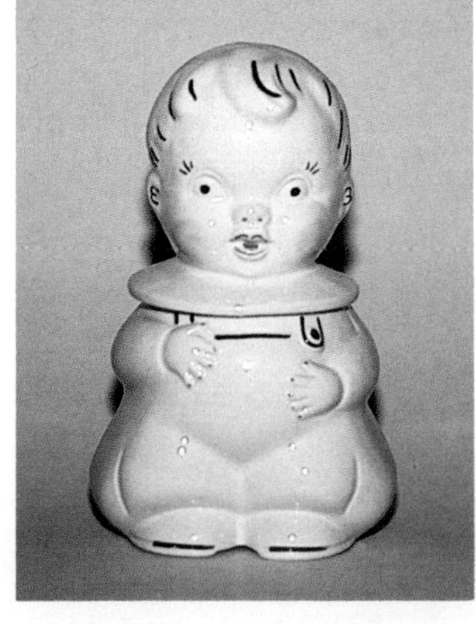

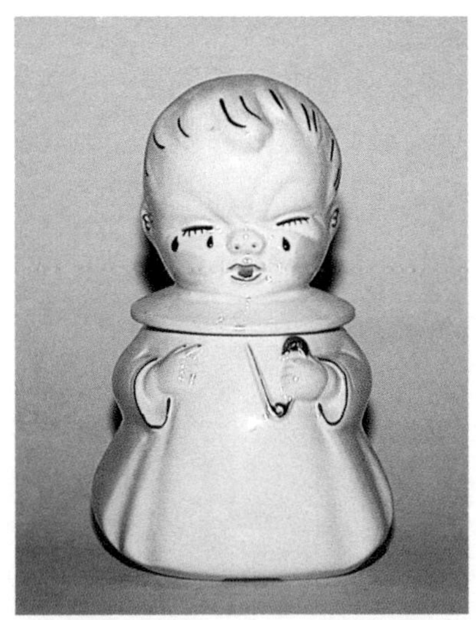

Joyce recently saw the turnabout baby with the lid fused on and a coin slot in the top of the head. It appeared to be a factory original.

Here is the cream of the crop in American Bisque.

ROW 1: *Wilma on Telephone,* "USA." "Flintstones" is written on the chair arm. $175.00-195.00

Fred Flintstone, "USA," "Flintstones" is impressed on the bottom of the base. $200.00-225.00

Rubbles House, "USA" $150.00-175.00

ROW 2: *Dino,* "USA." The actual production date is 1960. Stamp on bottom "Hanna-Barbera Productions copyright" $175.00-195.00

Dino Bank, "USA" on bottom $65.00-75.00

Fred and Wilma Bank, "USA" on bottom. On back, carved in "stone" is, "Fred loves Wilma." $65.00-75.00

Yogi Bear, "(C) Hanna-Barbera Productions Inc., 1961, USA" $100.00-105.00

ROW 3: *Casper* *, "Harvey Publications Inc., USA" $325.00-350.00

Popeye, "USA" $325.00-350.00

Olive Oyl, "USA" $425.00-450.00

Space Ship, "Cookies Out of this World, USA" $95.00-98.00

BELOW: *Little Audrey,* "USA" $400.00 & up

Little Audrey Bank, "USA" $65.00-75.00

Pages 44 and 45 show 1959 catalog sheets from American Bisque.

* **Collectors beware!** Authentic-looking reproductions of Casper have been appearing. These jars are being produced from a mold cast off of the original American Bisque cookie jar. Shrinkage occurs during this procedure leaving the finished product shorter than the original 13½" height. The jars will also weigh less than the original 5½ lb. weight.

CASPER
COOKIES OUT OF THIS WORLD

American Bisque Company

WILLIAMSTOWN, WEST VIRGINIA

1959 CATALOG
COOKIE JARS

CJ-708
COFFEE POT

CJ-711
CHURN

CJ-712
KITTENS & YARN

Packed assortment of your choice or 6 of an item to carton. Each jar individually boxed, 6 to master carton.

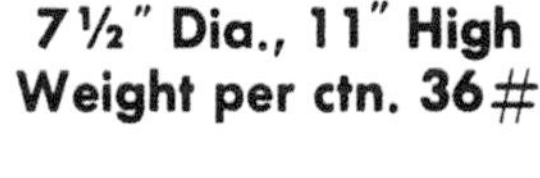

7½" Dia., 11" High
Weight per ctn. 36#

CJ-713
KITTEN & BEEHIVE

CJ-715
CLOWN

American Bisque Company

WILLIAMSTOWN, WEST VIRGINIA

1959 CATALOG COOKIE JARS

CJ-704
CHICK

CJ-705
BEAR

CJ-753
JACK IN BOX

Packed assortment of your choice or 6 of an item to carton. Each jar individually boxed, 6 to master carton.

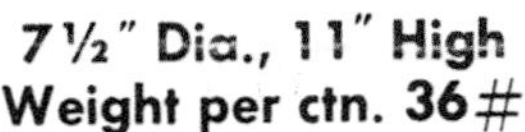

7½" Dia., 11" High
Weight per ctn. 36#

CJ-701
COLLEGIATE-OWL

CJ-702
MAGIC BUNNY

CJ-703
PIG-IN-POKE

Black Americana

Black Americana is the most competitive area of cookie jar collecting today. This field of collecting is very wide-ranged and the cookie jars are in especially high demand when collectors of general cookie jars are brought into play against collectors of black cookie jars.

Brayton Laguna

The Brayton Laguna Pottery Company was founded in Laguna Beach, California, in 1927, by Durlin Brayton. The company was run by Brayton until his death in 1951, and due to his incorporation of the business, it continued to run until the 1960's.

Pearl China

Pearl China, although now known as a pottery outlet, did indeed operate as a pottery at one time. Due to the expense involved in backstamping, the earliest items are unmarked. Eventually, however, their items were marked, sometimes very elaborately in gold.

Mosaic Tile

The original patent for what is commonly called the *Mosaic Tile Mammy* was issued in 1943 to Kenneth Gale in Zanesville, Ohio. It has never been determined whether the Mosaic Tile Company purchased the patent and produced the jar, or whether it was manufactured by another company and Mosaic Tile just received the credit.

ROW 1: *Brayton Mammy,* "Brayton Laguna Pottery, copyright." The *Brayton Mammy* is available in several colors. $200.00-225.00

Brayton salt and pepper shakers. The *Mammy* shaker is stamped "Brayton, California USA." $30.00-35.00

Brayton Mandy Planter, "Brayton, copyright," incised. "Mandy" is ink-stamped. $40.00-45.00

Brayton salt and pepper, marked as above. When we were offered these sets of salt and pepper shakers, we envisioned miniatures of the cookie jar with a mate to equal her; there isn't even a slight resemblance. $30.00-35.00

Polka Dot Mammy of unknown origin, unmarked $225.00-250.00

ROW 2: *Pearl China Chef,* "Cooky" on chest, "Pearl China Co., Hand Decorated 22 kt. gold 639." $250.00-275.00

Pearl China salt and pepper, range size, "Salty and Peppy" in gold, otherwise unmarked $80.00-90.00

Pearl China salt and pepper, small, "Salty and Peppy" in gold, otherwise unmarked $50.00-60.00

Pearl China Watermelon Mammy, unmarked $400.00 & up

Pearl China Mammy, mate to *Chef,* "Mammy" on front. Our jar is unmarked, but some are marked on the bottom with a gold stamp under the glaze. $400.00-425.00

ROW 3: *Mosaic Tile Mammy,* unmarked $150.00-175.00

Luzianne Mammy, plastic salt and pepper. This was produced in the early 1950's for the Luzianne Coffee Company by the F&F Mold and Die Works Company. The original set is in green and is marked "Luzianne Mammy, F&F Mold and Die Works, Dayton, Ohio. Made in U.S.A." $70.00-80.00

Luzianne Mammy pottery cookie jar. The only identifying mark on the original jar is "USA," written in script on its bottom. The original jar is also cold paint, not under the glaze, so most of the jars show paint wear to some degree. The *Luzianne Mammy* is currently being reproduced from the original mold, so beware. There are also pottery salt and pepper shakers to match the original jar which are being reproduced as well. $375.00-400.00

Luzianne Coffee Tin $35.00-40.00

Mosaic Tile Mammy, unmarked $150.00-175.00

LUZIANNE
DARK
ROAST
PURE
COFFEE
WM. B. REILY & COMPANY, Inc.
NEW ORLEANS, U.S.A.

ROW 1: *Aunt Jemima Cookie Jar,* unmarked. This is the second cookie jar offered as a premium by Quaker Oats. This soft-molded plastic jar is smaller than the original, and the skin is a much lighter brown. $100.00-110.00

Basket Handle Mammy, stamped "Japan" $235.00-240.00

Stringholder, "Japan" stamped inside $65.00-75.00

Mammy and Butler salt and pepper shakers, "Japan" $50.00-55.00

Butler, stamped "Made in Japan" $375.00-385.00

ROW 2: *Basket Handle Mammy,* "Maruhon Ware (K), Hand Painted, Japan" $195.00-205.00

Cream of Wheat Chef, stamped "Japan." This bears an amazing similarity to the advertising symbol used by the Cream of Wheat cereal. $150.00-160.00

Candy Jar, or possible salesman sample, unmarked $70.00-75.00

Little Girl, "Copyright Sears Roebuck and Co., 1978 Japan" $350.00-360.00

ROW 3: *Chef's Head,* unmarked $40.00-50.00

Salt and Pepper to match chef's head, unmarked $20.00-25.00

Rockingham Mammy, unmarked, approximate production date early 1980's. Rockingham also made a black clown of a very similar design to the Mammy, paper label on Dianne Cauwell's reads, "SARSAPARILLA DECODESIGNS N.Y.C. N.Y. copyright 1980 Japan." $140.00-150.00

New Orleans Mammy. This bisque jar was produced in the early 1980's. "T.M." is stamped on the back below the bow. Some of these jars are found with "New Orleans" printed on the front, and some just have a squiggle. $140.00-150.00

Bell to match bisque *Mammy,* unmarked $15.00-20.00

Toothpick Holder to match bisque *Mammy,* unmarked $12.00-18.00

LEFT: *Mosaic Tile Mammy,* unmarked, rare color $300.00 & up

NEW ORLEANS
NEW ORLEANS

F&F

F & F or Fiedler and Fiedler Mold and Die Works Company of Dayton, Ohio, created the black promotional line for Quaker Oats, the parent company of Aunt Jemima pancakes.

The syrup pitcher was the first piece of the promotional line to be issued. It was born of a business luncheon between the F & F plant manager and a Quaker Oats representative. The design was sketched on the tablecloth during lunch, thereby creating the unforgettable image so popular with collectors today.

The original *Aunt Jemima* premium pieces had black painted faces and arms. At a later production date, brown paint was substituted for the black on the cookie jar only.

Production commenced in the early 1950's with the syrup pitcher. Pieces were added and production continued into the early 1960's when they were discontinued due to the possible racial controversy these pieces could create.

Each item in the original set is marked with the "F & F" logo on the bottom.

ROW 1: *Aunt Jemina* cookie jar, "F & F Mold & Die Works, Dayton, Ohio" $175.00-195.00

Aunt Jemima & Uncle Mose large salt and pepper, "F & F Mold & Die Works, Dayton, Ohio" $50.00-60.00

Cloth *Aunt Jemima* 100-pound sack $50.00-60.00

ROW 2: *Aunt Jemima* cookie jar, "F & F Mold & Die Works, Dayton, Ohio" $150.00-175.00

Aunt Jemima syrup pitcher, "F & F Mold & Die Works, Dayton, Ohio" $35.00-40.00

ROW 3: Small *Aunt Jemima and Uncle Mose* salt and pepper, "F & F Mold & Die Works, Dayton, Ohio" $25.00-30.00

Aunt Jemima and Uncle Mose creamer and sugar, "F & F Mold & Die Works, Dayton, Ohio" $75.00-85.00

Aunt Jemima recipe box, unmarked, not part of the original kitchen set $85.00-95.00

Spice Set: Each individual spice jar is marked "F & F Mold & Die Works, Dayton, Ohio." The rack is not marked and is not of the original set. If the spice set were in the original copper-plated rack, it would have an extended value. $250.00-265.00

NET WEIGHT
The Quaker Oats Company
ADDRESS CHICAGO, U.S.A
Ginger
Allspice
Cinnamon
Paprika
Cloves
Nutmeg

ROW 1:	*Mammy,* stamped "Made in Japan"	$225.00-250.00
	Salt and pepper, "Japan"	$65.00-75.00
	Chef mug, "Japan." Available in two sizes.	$30.00-35.00
	Chef, stamped "Made in Japan"	$200.00-225.00
ROW 2:	*National Silver Chef,* "NSCO"	$120.00-130.00
	National Silver Mammy, "NSCO USA." Although this pair of jars is marked NSCO, they were actually made by another pottery for the National Silver Company, since National Silver is merely a selling agency.	$120.00-130.00
	Mammy, unmarked, with the exception of the original price of $1.19.	$120.00-130.00
	Chef, unmarked	$85.00-95.00
ROW 3:	*Mammy,* handmade, marked "To R J, 1941"	$70.00-80.00
	Mammy, unmarked, totally flat, unglazed bottom	$65.00-70.00
	Chef, unmarked, totally flat, unglazed bottom. We have found the first one with a large amount of the original paint on the face, arms, and buttons; however, it is not pictured here. This jar was produced in the 1930's to 1940's.	$60.00-70.00
	Salt and pepper, unmarked	$18.00-22.00
BELOW:	The wonderful *Washtub Mammy.*	$400.00 & up

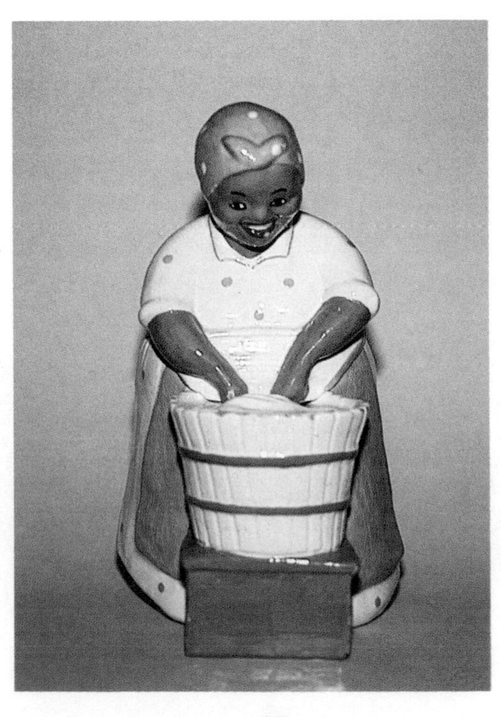

ROW 1:	*Mammy,* "McCoy," (1948-57). This is the only yellow Mammy we've ever seen painted and believe it is original. The solid color Mammies are much harder to find than the white ones.	$250.00-260.00
	Mammy, "McCoy"(1948-57)	$200.00-225.00
	Mammy, "McCoy" (1948-57)	$145.00-155.00
ROW 2:	*Mammy,* "copyright, MANN"	$250.00-260.00
	Mammy, "McCoy" (1948-57)	$250.00-260.00
ROW 3:	*Chef,* "Artistic Potteries, Inc., California," believed to be in business in the 1940's in Whittier, California	$75.00-80.00
	Cauliflower Mammy, "McCoy USA" (1939)	$400.00-450.00
	Chef, "Artistic Potteries, Inc., California"	$75.00-80.00
BELOW:	*Mammy* cookie jar, "Weller"	$500.00-600.00
	Mammy teapot, "Weller"	$400.00-450.00
	Mammy syrup pitcher, "Weller"	$300.00-325.00
	Mammy batter bowl, "Weller"	$400.00-450.00

Cookies
Cookies

Cookies

Cookies

Rick Wisecarver Originals

Rick Wisecarver has established a reputation for his beautiful hand painted, sculptured art pottery. Rick began his art work painting on canvas when he was 17 years old. The family moved to Roseville, Ohio, where his mother started a ceramic shop. There he was encouraged by her to try his art work on pottery vases. Rick had developed an interest in the old Weller and Roseville pottery, so he began to experiment with clays and glazes until he was able to duplicate the old methods. It was in his mother's ceramic shop that Rick achieved his goal.

In 1983, he began a series of Classic Cookie Jars that have become quite collectible. All are originals, designed and sculptured by Rick with the molds made by his father. All authentic pieces are signed by Rick Wisecarver and are called WIHOA'S COOKIE CLASSIC. The "WI" represents Wisecarver; the "HO" is for his mother's maiden name of Hoadley; the "A" stands for Ault, Rick's cousin; the "S" is for his business partner, Richard Sims. Rick's Wihoa's Art Pottery is now found throughout the U.S.A.

Carol Gifford Originals

Carol Gifford was born and reared in Eureka, California. When she was a small child, Carol's mother gave her a McCoy *Aunt Jemima* jar that had been a gift of her and her father's. She cherished this little mammy for years and would admire her sitting on top of her mother's refrigerator.

After Carol married her husband Virgil, all three of their children wanted the little *Aunt Jemima* cookie jar. She set out to different flea markets hoping to find one for each of them. As Carol looked for these McCoy *Aunt Jemima* cookie jars, she noticed so many interesting collectibles in the "Black" line that she began to make this her hobby.

After collecting a full kitchen of nothing but Black collectibles, Carol decided to make her own design in a "mammy" cookie jar. She had done ceramics for about fifteen years and, with the help of an East Coast artist, they sculpted a *Watermelon Mammy.* The *Watermelon Mammy* was such a success that Carol decided to do a whole series of "Black" cookie jars. She was interested in the Black American heritage and wanted to proudly represent it. She has tried to make her cookie jar designs most exclusive and each jar of the utmost quality. The jars are painted under the glaze and trimmed in 24 karat gold. They are of a limited edition of 250 of each jar. Upon reaching this number, the molds are broken.

ROW 1: *Cookstove Mammy,* "Wihoa's Original Cookie Classic by Rick Wisecarver, R. Sims, Roseville, Ohio" (1988) $90.00-110.00

Mammy with Child, "Wihoa's Original Cookie Classic by Rick Wisecarver, copyright R. Sims 1989, Roseville,Ohio" $90.00-110.00

Young Black Woman, "Wihoa's Original Cookie Classic by Rick Wisecarver, copyright R. Sims 9/7/89 Roseville, Ohio 43777" $90.00-110.00

ROW 2: *Pancake Mammy,* "copyright 1987 CG Carol Gifford" $125.00-130.00

Butler, "copyright 1987 CG Carol Gifford" $125.00-130.00

Mixing Bowl Mammy, "Wihoa's Original Cookie Classic by Rick Wisecarver" (1983) $90.00-110.00

Cookie Jar Mammy, "Wihoa's Original Cookie Classic by Rick Wisecarver, copyright R. Sims 1984 Roseville, Ohio" $90.00-110.00

ROW 3: *Watermelon Mammy,* "copyright 1986 CG Carol Gifford" $125.00-130.00

Watermelon Sammy, "copyright 1987 CG Carol Gifford" $125.00-130.00

Rocking Chair Granny, "copyright 1987 CG Carol Gifford" $125.00-130.00

ROW 1: *Mammy,* medium-size, "Made in Taiwan." This cookie jar had to be patterned from the cast-iron bank. $25.00-30.00

Mammy, small, "Made in Taiwan." Note the resemblance to the *New Orleans Mammy.* $18.00-22.00

Mammy, ceramic F & F reproduction, "Made in Taiwan" $30.00-35.00

ROW 2: *Small Head Mammy,* "MEMORIES OF MAMA," registered trademark. This is a McCoy *Mammy* reproduction. $42.00-45.00

Small Head Mammy canister set, "MEMORIES OF MAMA," registered trademark. *Small Head Mammy* canister jar, second size, marked as above. *Small Head Mammy* canister jar, third in series. *Small Head Mammy* canister jar, fourth. $110.00-120.00

ROW 3: *Luzianne Mammy Reproduction,* unmarked $75.00-80.00

Large Head Mammy, "MEMORIES OF MAMA," registered trademark. This is a *Mosaic Tile Mammy* reproduction. Also available in the *Large Head* are salt and pepper, sugar and creamer, fruit jar lid (large and small), spoon caddy, napkin holder, lamp, and toothpick holder. $42.00-45.00

Large Head Mammy jam jar $30.00-32.00

Small Head Mammy jam jar $30.00-32.00

Small Head Mammy in red, marked as above. Also available in the *Small Head* are salt and pepper, sugar and creamer, fruit jar lid (small and large), and toothpick holder. $42.00-45.00

BELOW: *Mammy,* "Japan" $185.00-195.00

Mammy, Butler salt and pepper, unmarked $50.00-55.00

McCoy Lookalike, unmarked $185.00-195.00

McCoy Lookalike salt and pepper, unmarked $35.00-45.00

Cookies

ROW 1:	*Basket Handle Mammy,* "Mauhon Ware (K) Hand Painted, Japan"	$195.00-205.00
	Mammy Shaker with Spoon Rest (Gilner), unmarked	$75.00-85.00
	Gilner Mammy, unmarked	$350.00-375.00
	Mann Mammy, "copyright MANN"	$180.00-190.00
ROW 2:	*Mammy,* "Enesco Imports Japan"	$125.00-135.00
	Chef, "Enesco Imports Japan"	$125.00-135.00
	Plaid Apron Mammy, "Japan"	$150.00-160.00
ROW 3:	*Gold-Teeth Mammy,* unmarked. The base of this jar stands on shallow wedges, and from her appearance is possibly a fairly new jar. The price given is the actual amount paid for the jar in 1987.	$290.00-300.00
	Spice, unmarked Treasure Craft	$35.00-45.00
	Fallcreek Mammy, "Fallcreek Ceramics"	$25.00-30.00

ROW 1: Metlox *Mammy,* "Original Calif. Pottery by Metlox, copyright by Vincent" $85.00-95.00

Mammy and Chef salt and pepper, unmarked but also by Metlox. $40.00-45.00

Red or Metlox *Mammy,* "Original Calif. Pottery by Metlox, copyright by Vincent." The *Red Mammy* appears to be the harder color to locate. $100.00-125.00

Mammy and Chef salt and pepper, unmarked but also by Metlox. $50.00-55.00

Metlox *Mammy,* "Original Calif. Pottery by Metlox, copyright by Vincent" $85.00-95.00

Mammy and Chef salt and pepper, unmarked but alsoby Metlox $40.00-45.00

ROW 2: *Mandy* cookie jar, "copyright Omnibus Japan" $55.00-65.00

Picaninny salt and pepper, unmarked but also by Omnibus $18.00-22.00

Mandy pitcher, "copyright Omnibus Japan" $55.00-65.00

Mandy teapot, "copyright Omnibus Japan" $55.00-65.00

Mandy sugar and *Flower* creamer, "copyright OCI Japan" $25.00-30.00

ROW 3: *Topsy,* "Metlox, Calif. USA" $85.00-95.00

Black Santa, "Original Calif. Pottery by Metlox" $115.00-125.00

Polka Dot Topsy, "Metlox, Calif. USA." Topsy is available in yellow trim and red trim. $85.00-95.00

BELOW: *Basket Handle Mammy Head,* unmarked $195.00-205.00

Mini-Teapot salt and pepper, unmarked $45.00-50.00

Brush

The Brush cookie jars were produced for approximately 25 years, from 1946 through 1971.

Brush had two main designers for its cookie jar line. The "W" mark, found on so many of our favorites, stands for the twin brothers, Don and Ross Winton.

Several of the Brush jars have been found with gold trim, which adds to their desirability.

ROW 1:	*Stylized Siamese,* "W/41" (1967)	$65.00-75.00
	Treasure Chest, "W/28" (1962)	$65.00-75.00
	Stylized Owl, "W/42" (1967)	$65.00-75.00
ROW 2:	*Crock with Duck Finial,* "K/26, USA" (1956)	$25.00-35.00
	Crock with Cat Finial, "K/26, USA" (1956)	$25.00-35.00
	Crock with Little Girl Praying, "K/26, USA" (1956)	$25.00-35.00
ROW 3:	*Cookie House,* "W/31" (1962)	$40.00-45.00
	Three Bears, "K/2, Brush USA" (1962)	$40.00-45.00
	Old Shoe, "W/23, Brush USA" (1959)	$50.00-55.00

COOKIES
COOKIES
COOKIES

ROW 1:	*Donkey and Cart,* "W/33 Brush USA" (1965)	$115.00-125.00
	Squirrel with Top Hat, "W/15 USA," early 1950's	$80.00-85.00
	Donkey and Cart, "W/33 Brush USA" (1965)	$115.00-125.00
ROW 2:	*Teddy Bear* (with feet together), "014 USA" (1957)	$85.00-90.00
	Panda, "W21 BRUSH USA" (1957)	$90.00-95.00
	Teddy Bear (with feet apart), "W 14 USA," early 1950's	$80.00-85.00
ROW 3:	*Happy Bunny,* "W 25 Brush USA" (1965)	$70.00-75.00
	Squirrel with Top Hat, "W 15 USA," early 1950's	$80.00-85.00
	Happy Bunny, "W 25 Brush USA" (1960)	$70.00-75.00
BELOW:	*Hillbilly Frog,* "43D" (1969)	$300.00 & up

ROW 1:	Small *Little Boy Blue,* gold trim, "K 25 USA" (1956)	$175.00-200.00
	Small *Little Boy Blue,* plain, "K 25 USA " (1956)	$125.00-150.00
	Mug, unmarked (1956)	$30.00-40.00
	Large *Little Boy Blue,* "K 24, Brush USA" (1956). The number "K 24" has to be a factory error, but it is the actual mark on the jar.	$125.00-150.00
ROW 2:	*Davey Crocket,* gold trim, "USA" (1956)	$155.00-165.00
	Small *Little Red Riding Hood,* "K 24, USA" (1956)	$125.00-150.00
	Large *Little Red Riding Hood,* "K 24, Brush USA" (1956)	$125.00-150.00
ROW 3:	*Davey Crocket,* "USA" (1956)	$75.00-90.00
	Mug, unmarked (1956)	$30.00-40.00
	Small *Peter Pan,* "USA" (1956)	$125.00-150.00
	Large *Peter Pan,* "K 23 Brush USA" (1956)	$125.00-150.00

BELOW LEFT TO RIGHT:

Panda, "W 21, Brush USA" (1959)	$150.00-175.00
Peter Pan, gold trim, "USA" (1956)	$225.00-250.00
Mug, gold trim, unmarked (1956)	$65.00-75.00
Boy and Balloons, unmarked (1971)	$250.00-275.00

DAVY
CROCKETT

ROW 1: *Clown,* "W 22," Brush USA $80.00-85.00

Clown, "W 22, Brush USA" (1964) $75.00-80.00

Clown, "W 22, Brush USA" (1965). There are at least four color versions in the standing *Clown.* The *Clown* with brown pants, not shown, appears to be the oldest, produced in 1957. $75.00-80.00

ROW 2: *Formal Pig,* "W 7, USA" $85.00-95.00

Formal Pig with gold trim, "W 7 USA" $100.00-125.00

Formal Pig, "W 7, USA" (1965). There are also several color variations in the *Formal Pig.* The black coat and hat were produced through 1956. $85.00-95.00

ROW 3: *Humpty Dumpty* with Peaked Hat, "W 29 Brush USA" (1962) $70.00-75.00

Humpty Dumpty with Beanie and Bow Tie, "W 18 Brush USA." The beanie, bow tie *Humpty* was produced from 1956 through 1961. $75.00-80.00

Humpty Dumpty with Peaked Hat, "W 29 Brush USA" (1962) $75.00-80.00

ROW 1:	*Granny,* "W 19 Brush USA" (1957)	$75.00-80.00
	Circus Horse, unmarked, early 1950's	$175.00-195.00
	Granny, "W 19 Brush USA." The plain skirt was produced in 1956.	$75.00-80.00
ROW 2:	*Laughing Hippo,* "W 27 Brush USA" (1961)	$150.00-175.00
	Elephant (wearing baby hat) "W 8 USA," early 1950's	$120.00-130.00
	Sitting Hippo, unmarked (1969)	$115.00-125.00
ROW 3:	*Chick and Nest,* "W 38 Brush USA" (1966)	$115.00-125.00
	Hobby Horse, unmarked (1971)	$225.00-250.00
	Hen on Basket, unmarked (1969)	$70.00-75.00

Brush was not consistent in its cookie jar design, which sometimes makes identification difficult. Some of its jars were produced with a standard dry foot and were clearly marked; others, such as the *Laughing Hippo,* the *Hen on Basket,* and the *Clown Bust* had wedges on the bases and were unmarked.

Although the designs varied, the quality did not, and the Brush jars are highly sought after by collectors.

ROW 1:	*Cow with Cat Finial,* "W 10 Brush USA," early 1950's	$65.00-70.00
	Cow with Cat Finial, "W 10 Brush USA," early 1950's	$250.00 & up
	Cow with Cat Finial, "W 10 Brush USA."	$65.00-70.00
ROW 2:	*Puppy Police,* "W 39 Brush USA" (1966)	$215.00-225.00
	Elephant (wearing baby hat), "W 8 USA," early 1950's	$120.00-130.00
	Sitting Pig, "W 37 Brush USA" (1966)	$115.00-125.00
ROW 3:	*Nite Owl,* "W 40" (1967)	$70.00-75.00
	Squirrel on Log, "USA" (1965)	$50.00-55.00
	Dog with Basket, unmarked (1971)	$55.00-60.00

ROW 1:	*Cinderella Pumpkin,* "W 32 Brush USA" (1967)	$75.00-80.00
	Covered Wagon, "W 30 Brush USA" (1962)	$175.00-185.00
	Cinderella Pumpkin, "W 32 Brush USA" (1962)	$75.00-80.00
ROW 2:	*Squirrel on Log,* "USA" (1969)	$50.00-55.00
	Pumpkin with Lock on Door, "W 24 USA," discontinued in 1961.	$100.00-110.00
	Squirrel on Log, "USA" (1961). Notice the three production dates for the *Squirrel on Log.* The colors pin point the production dates.	$50.00-55.00
ROW 3:	*Cow with Cat Finial,* "W 10 Brush USA" (1970)	$200.00 & up
	Cookie House, "W 31 Brush USA" (1962)	$40.00-45.00
	Antique Touring Car, unmarked (1971)	$125.00-135.00

ROW 1:	*Raggedy Ann,* "W 16 USA" (1956)	$95.00-105.00
	Little Angel, "Brush USA" (1956)	$225.00-250.00
	Little Girl, "017 Brush USA" (1957)	$95.00-105.00
ROW 2:	*Cherry Jar,* "H 5 Brush USA"	$25.00-30.00
	Circus Horse, unmarked, early 1950's	$175.00-195.00
	Clown Bust, unmarked (1970)	$95.00-105.00
ROW 3:	*Old Clock,* "W 20 Brush USA" (1956). This delightful poem is engraved on the sides: "It's cookie time the clock around. You'll find you eat them by the pound. Tick Tock the cookie clock - To help yourself just lift the top."	$65.00-75.00
	Red Riding Hood, large, gold-trimmed, "K 24 Brush USA" (1956)	$250.00-275.00
	Mug, unmarked	$50.00-60.00
	Lantern, "K 1 Brush USA"	$40.00-45.00

11 12 1
10 2
9 3
8 4
7 6 5

ROW 1: *Cow with Cat Finial,* "W 10" (1970) — $400.00 & up

Owl, unmarked, unusual horseshoe-shaped foot (1965) — $100.00-115.00

Fish, unmarked (1971) — $115.00-125.00

ROW 2: *Raggedy Ann,* "W 16 USA" (1956) — $145.00-155.00

Red Riding Hood, unmarked except on skirt, "Littl Red Ridding Hood" (sic) (1956) — $250.00-275.00

Little Girl, "USA Brush." Note the birds on her skirt. — $145.00-155.00

ROW 3: *Smiling Bear,* unmarked, sits on wedges like the green hippo — $165.00-175.00

Elephant (wearing baby hat) "W 8 USA," early 1950's — $175.00-195.00

Sitting Piggy Bank, "837 USA Brush." Apparently the "W" was dropped on the bank, and the "8" added to the "37." "W 37" marks the *Sitting Piggy* cookie jar. — $105.00-115.00

Brush produced banks from several of its cookie jar molds. Joyce has seen the formal pig with a birth announcement under the glaze, undoubtedly a gift from a Brush employee.

BELOW: *Raggedy Ann,* "W 16 USA" — $115.00-125.00

California Originals

California Originals was established in the 1940's in Torrence, California, by William D. Bailey. In 1979, Harold Roman purchased the company to combine with his present holdings of Roman Ceramics and Cumberland Ware. It was during this era California Originals was licensed by Walt Disney, Walter Lantz, D.C. Comics, Muppets, etc. to produce the fantastic cartoon characters so highly sought after by today's collectors. California Originals was closed in 1982.

ROW 1:	*Superman,* "copyright, D.C. Comics, Inc., 1978 Calif. Original USA 846," also available in brown	$150.00-175.00
	Big Bird, "copyright, MUPPETS INC., 976"	$35.00-40.00
	Wonder Woman, "USA 847, copyright, D.C. Comics Inc., 1978"	$175.00-200.00
ROW 2:	*Big Bird,* "copyright, MUPPETS INC., 971"	$35.00-40.00
	Ernie and Bert Fine Cookies, "977, copyright 1971, 1978 MUPPETS INC.,"	$65.00-75.00
	The Count, "975"	$90.00-110.00
ROW 3:	*Ernie,* "copyright MUPPETS INC., 973"	$35.00-40.00
	Cookie Monster, "copyright, MUPPETS INC., 970"	$35.00-40.00
	Oscar the Grouch, "copyright, MUPPETS INC., 972"	$35.00-40.00

SUPERMAN
TELEPHONE
COOKIES
Wonder Woman
COOKIE
BANK

ERNIE AND BERT
FINE COOKIES

ROW 1:	*Frog with Bow Tie,* "2645, USA"	$25.00-30.00
	Crawling Turtle, "2728, USA"	$20.00-25.00
	Owl, "2751, USA," also produced with Cumberland Ware mark	$20.00-25.00
ROW 2:	*Beaver,* "2625"	$25.00-30.00
	Sitting Turtle, "2635, USA"	$20.00-25.00
	Mouse, "2630, USA"	$20.00-25.00
ROW 3:	*Small Owl,* "856, USA"	$18.00-22.00
	Bear, "2648, USA"	$18.00-22.00
	Mushroom on Stump, "2956"	$18.00-22.00

ROW 1: *Dog on Stump,* "2620" $18.00-22.00

Small Squirrel on Stump, "2620, C" $15.00-18.00

Large Squirrel on Stump, "2620" $18.00-22.00

ROW 2: *Cat on Safe,* "2630" $18.00-22.00

White Rabbit, paper label: "California Originals" $30.00-35.00

Sitting Cat on Safe, "2630" $18.00-22.00

ROW 3: *Pelican*, unmarked $30.00-35.00

Elf School House, unmarked $18.00-22.00

Elephant, "2643, USA" $18.00-22.00

BELOW: *Koala Bear,* unmarked. This particular cookie jar is not Regal China as believed to be by some collectors. There are several matching accessories to this great jar. $110.00-125.00

Woody Woodpecker, "copyright Walter Lantz Prod. Inc. 980 USA" $125.00-150.00

COOKIE
SAFE
COOKIE
SAFE

ROW 1:	*Bear,* "G-405"	$18.00-25.00
	Clown on Elephant, "896"	$18.00-25.00
	Dog, "458"	$18.00-25.00
ROW 2:	*Santa Claus,* "871" impressed in reverse on back	$50.00-60.00
	Christmas Tree, unmarked	$75.00-85.00
	Yellow Cab, unmarked	$45.00-50.00
ROW 3:	*W.C. Fields,* "Cumberland Ware." The mark is a "C" through a "W."	$75.00-85.00
	Monk, "Cumberland Ware." The mark is a "C" through a "W."	$30.00-35.00
	Sailor Mouse, "Cumberland Ware." The mark is a "C" through a "W."	$30.00-35.00
BELOW:	*Stan Laurel,* "C" through "W"	$75.00-85.00
	Koala Bear, "C" through "W"	$55.00-65.00

RADIO
DISPATCHED
TAXI

Thou shalt
not steal

These copies of 8" x 10" photos of the *R2-D2, Darth Vader,* and *C-3PO* banks by Roman Ceramics, the *Stan Laurel, Oliver Hardy,* and *W.C. Fields* by Cumberland Ware, and the Koala Bear by California Originals were sent to us by Harold Roman from his files after the closing of these companies. No doubt they were to be used in a promotional campaign.

These additional copies of photos are from Harold Roman's California Originals files.

TOP LEFT: Pictured at the top is a delicious-looking, but inedible *Cupcake.* Pictured below it, smiling big, is a very bright colored *Clown.* Both are done by California Originals.

TOP RIGHT: Sitting together we have quite a team. There is an adorable little *Tiger* sitting atop his mountain, just daring someone for a challenge. Next, we have a very plump Frog who is looking high up into the sky for his next victim to fly by.

BOTTOM RIGHT: Seeing these items makes one want to run up and give them a quick hug. Not only do we have the cookie jar in the form of the adorable Koala Bear, there are also matching accessories including salt and pepper shakers, a planter, and a bank.

Cardinal

The Cardinal China Company was a distributor located in Carteret, New Jersey. According to a letter from Gary R. Darwin, Vice President of Sales for Cardinal in 1981, these jars were contracted and made by American Bisque Corporation in Williamstown, West Virginia. He further stated that Cardinal had manufactured many, many years before it began importing, but cookie jars were not made in their kilns.

ROW 1:	*Little Girl,* "Cardinal USA 301"	$50.00-55.00
	Garage, "Cardinal USA 306"	$38.00-42.00
	Pig, "Cardinal USA 304"	$38.00-42.00
ROW 2:	*Clown,* "Cardinal USA 302"	$40.00-45.00
	Smart Cookie, "Cardinal USA 303"	$45.00-50.00
	French Chef, "Cardinal USA 305"	$45.00-50.00
ROW 3:	*Telephone,* "Cardinal USA 311"	$30.00-35.00
	Castle, "Cardinal USA 307"	$35.00-40.00
	Soldier, "Cardinal USA 312." The *Soldier* is also available with a bank in the lid.	$50.00-55.00

All of these jars were found in an old catalog sheet dated 1958.

The missing numbers in the above sequence are "308"-*Cookie Bus,* "309"-*Cookie Safe,* and "310"-*Cookie Sack* with cookies on the lid.

Cookies
Free Parking For Cookies
So ahead
Make a pig
of yourself

I
Want
Some

Doranne of California

Doranne of California was established in 1951 in Los Angeles, California, by Irving Dietz. Doranne is still in business today, but only produces two cookie jars, the *Fire Hydrant* and the *Garbage Can,* which are sold in large-volume orders to specialized customers.

ROW 1:	*Cow on Moon,* "J 2, USA," produced in the late 1950's	$75.00-80.00
	Cat with Bow Tie, "J 5, USA"	$35.00-40.00
	Elephant, "16 USA"	$35.00-38.00
ROW 2:	*Lion,* "K O 3, USA." The numbering on the *Lion* is different, but the characteristics all match typical Doranne.	$35.00-38.00
	Camel, "J 8 USA"	$35.00-40.00
	Hippo, "USA," produced in the late 1950's. The similarity to the Brush *Hippo* is amazing.	$70.00-75.00
ROW 3:	*Bear,* "J 7 USA"	$30.00-35.00
	Fish, "J 9 USA"	$35.00-40.00
	Mother Goose, "C J 16 USA," produced in the late 1960's	$65.00-70.00

ROW 1:	*Ketchup Bottle,* "C J 68 USA," produced in 1984	$35.00-38.00
	Fire Hydrant, "C J 50," produced 1984-present	$35.00-38.00
	Cookie Cola, "C J 67 USA," produced in 1984	$35.00-38.00
ROW 2:	*Elephant,* "Calif. 15 USA"	$28.00-32.00
	Cat, "J 5 USA"	$28.00-32.00
	Hound Dog, "J 1 USA"	$30.00-35.00
ROW 3:	*Green Pepper,* "C J 30 USA," produced in 1984	$25.00-28.00
	Peanut, "C J 18 USA"	$25.00-28.00
	Seal, "USA 17"	$25.00-28.00

Below: An original Doranne of California catalog sheet from the 1980's. Take note of the *Garbage Can* which is one of only two cookie jars being produced by Doranne today.

"Farmyard Follies"

ROW 1:	*Hen with Basket of Eggs,* "C J - 103" (1984)	$38.00-42.00
	Duck with Basket of Corn, "C J - 104" (1984)	$38.00-42.00
	Pig with Barrel of Pork, "C J - 105" (1984)	$38.00-42.00
ROW 2:	*Cow with Can of Milk,* "C J - 107" (1984)	$38.00-42.00
	Rabbit with Carrot, "C J - 106" (1984)	$38.00-42.00
	Donkey with Sack of Oats, "C J - 108" (1984)	$38.00-42.00
ROW 3:	*Owl,* "J H, USA"	$22.00-28.00
	Hen, "C J - 100"	$22.00-28.00
	Monkey, "C J - 21"	$22.00-28.00

Below is a catalog sheet from Doranne of California supplied to their customers in the 1980's. Pages 100 and 101 feature additional catalog sheets.

FARMYARD FOLLIES
CJ104
CJ102
CJ103
CJ107
CJ106
CJ100
SW100
CJ108
CJ105
CJ102L

CALIFORNIA COOKIE JARS
DISCONTINUED
J65S
J 67 C
J66C
J57A
LAS VEGAS
JACKPOT
DISCONTINUED
DISCONTINUED
DISCONTINUED
DISCONTINUED
DISCONTINUED
J 48 B
DISCONTINUED
BROWN
BAGGER
J71B
J54C
J55C

ROW 1:	*Cow on Moon*, "J 2 USA"	$60.00-65.00

Fredericksburg Art Pottery Co.

FAPCO operated in Fredericksburg, Ohio, from 1939-1948. The Fredericksburg Art Pottery Company was co-founded by John T. McLane and George Heisler and was run jointly until its closing.

ROW 1:	*Bear*, marked "F.A.P.Co."	$35.00-40.00
	Bear, marked "F.A.P.Co."	$35.00-40.00
ROW 2:	*Hen*, "F.A.P.Co. USA"	$20.00-25.00
	Bartender, "USA"	$40.00-45.00
	Hen, "F.A.P.Co. USA"	$20.00-25.00
ROW 3:	*Windmill*, "F.A.P.Co."	$20.00-25.00
	Dove, "F.A.P.Co. USA"	$25.00-30.00
	Windmill, "F.A.P.Co."	$20.00-25.00

Gilner

No information is available, but Gilner is believed to have been a California-based company.

Row 1: *Rooster,* "Gilner, G-22" $28.00-32.00

Bear, "Gilner, G-405"' $28.00-32.00

Gonder Art Pottery

Gonder Art Pottery was produced in Zanesville, Ohio, from 1941 until 1955, at which time production was changed entirely to the manufacture of tile, due again to competition from foreign imports.

The Gonder *Sheriff* cookie jar is unique in its mold design of two separate legs, whereas most designs blend the leg shapes together for production ease.

ROW 1: *Sheriff,* "Gonder Original, 950" $225.00-250.00

Hull

The Hull Pottery Company, originally known as the A.E. Hull Pottery Company, was located in Crooksville, Ohio, from 1905 until 1986. Hull's greatest fame lies in its patented design, *Little Red Riding Hood.* Pictured below is *Little Boy Blue,* a little-known, but extremely collectible, Hull cookie jar. For in-depth information of Hull Pottery, consult the *Collector's Encyclopedia of Hull Pottery* by Brenda Roberts, a fellow Missourian.

ROW 2: *Gingerbread Boy,* "Hull, copyright, Crooksville, Ohio, USA, Ovenproof" $30.00-35.00

Gingerbread Boy, marked as above $30.00-35.00

Gingerbread Boy, also marked as above $30.00-35.00

ROW 3: *Duck,* "Hull 966, USA" $28.00-32.00

Cookie Crock, "Hull Oven Proof, USA" $18.00-22.00

Daisy, "Hull 48" $18.00-22.00

BELOW: *Pirate,* unmarked, but believed to be Gonder $300.00 & up

Little Boy Blue, "Hull Ware Boy Blue, USA 971 $400.00 & up

Cookies

The A.E. Hull Company was established in 1905 in Crooksville, Ohio. Foremost to cookie jar collectors is their *Red Riding Hood* cookie jar which was patented in 1943. While Hull owned the patent rights, much of the *Red Riding Hood* collection was actually produced by Regal China in Antioch, Illinois.

The Hull Company discontinued its operations in 1986 after establishing a legend.

ROW 1:	*Milk Pitcher*, "Pat. Design 135889" (Regal)	$95.00-110.00
	Cracker Jar, unmarked (Regal)	$185.00-195.00
	Teapot, "USA" (Regal)	$90.00-100.00
ROW 2:	*Butter Dish*, "Pat. Design 135889" (Regal)	$165.00-175.00
	Salt Canister, "Pat. Design 135889" (Regal). Other canisters available are *Cereal, Coffee, Flour, Sugar, Tea, Potato Chips, Popcorn, Pretzels*, and *Tidbits*. The prices vary with rarity.	$300.00-325.00
	Mug, unmarked (Regal)	$175.00-200.00
	Planter, wall hanging, "Pat. Design 135889" (Regal)	$185.00-195.00
ROW 3:	*Salt and Pepper Shakers*, small, unmarked (Regal)	$25.00-30.00
	Salt and Pepper Shakers, rare, medium-size, "Pat. Design 135889" (Regal)	$175.00-195.00
	Salt and Pepper Shakers, unmarked (Regal)	$35.00-45.00
	Match Safe, wall hanging, "Pat. Design 135889" (Regal)	$400.00-425.00
ROW 4:	*Crawling Sugar*, unmarked (Regal)	$50.00-55.00
	Tab Creamer, unmarked (Regal)	$50.00-55.00
	Covered Sugar, "Pat. Design 135889" (Regal)	$115.00-125.00
	Creamer, "Pat. Design 135889" (Regal)	$75.00-85.00
	Open Sugar, "Pat. Design 135889" (Regal)	$35.00-40.00
	Open Sugar, "Pat. Design 135889" (Regal)	$35.00-40.00
BELOW:	*Spice Jars*, each marked "Pat. Design 135889" (Regal)	each $275.00-285.00

SALT

ROW 1:	*Little Red Riding Hood* with open basket, "Little Red Riding Hood Pat. Design 135889" (Regal)	$85.00-95.00
	Large *Salt* and *Pepper,* unmarked (Regal)	$40.00-45.00
	Little Red Riding Hood with full skirt, "Little Red Riding Hood Pat. Design 135889 USA" (Regal)	$150.00-160.00
	Salt and Pepper, small, unmarked (Regal)	$25.00-30.00
	Little Red Riding Hood with closed, basket, "Little Red Riding Hood Pat. Designs 135889" (Regal)	$85.00-95.00
ROW 2:	*Little Red Riding Hood,* "967 Hull Ware, Little Red Riding Hood"	$65.00-75.00
	Little Red Riding Hood, "967 Hull Ware, Little Red Riding Hood Pat. applied for USA"	$80.00-90.00
	Salt and Pepper, medium, "Pat. Design 135889" (Regal)	$175.00-195.00
	Little Red Riding Hood, "967 Hull Ware, Little Red Riding Hood Pat. applied for USA"	$85.00-90.00
ROW 3:	*Little Red Riding Hood,* "Little Red Riding Hood, Pat. Design 135889" (Regal)	$85.00-90.00
	Salt and Pepper, large, unmarked (Regal)	$40.00-45.00
	Little Red Riding Hood biscuit jar, "Pat. Design 135889 (Regal)	$185.00-195.00
	Salt and Pepper, small, unmarked (Regal)	$25.00-30.00
	Barefoot Boy, "Blessing on the Barefoot Boy." Produced by Gem Refractories for Hull	$190.00-195.00
BELOW:	*Red Riding Hood* lamp, "Pat. Design 135889" (Regal)	$650.00-700.00
	Wolf Jar, unmarked	$385.00-395.00
	Little Red Riding Hood, made by Gem Refractories	$100.00 & up

Japan

ROW 1:	*Pig with Little Pig Finial,* "Japan"	$15.00-18.00
	Tom and Jerry, "copyright, Metro Goldwyn Mayer Film Co. 1981," also paper label: "From the gift world of Gorham, Made in Japan"	$60.00-70.00
	Tom and Jerry, marked exactly as above	$60.00-70.00
ROW 2:	*Pig Chef,* "Japan"	$25.00-28.00
	Horse Doctor, "Japan"	$25.00-28.00
	Farmer Cow, "Japan"	$25.00-28.00
ROW 3:	*Fishing Hippo,* "Japan"	$25.00-28.00
	Hunting Dog, "Japan"	$25.00-28.00
	Climbing Bear, "Japan"	$25.00-28.00

ROW 1:	*Alice in Wonderland,* "Japan"	$50.00-55.00
	Dog with Cookie, "Japan"	$15.00-18.00
	Humpty Dumpty, "Japan"	$30.00-35.00
ROW 2:	*Bear with Cookie,* "Japan"	$25.00-28.00
	Horse Mechanic, "Japan"	$25.00-28.00
	Chipmonk, "Japan 2863"	$25.00-28.00
ROW 3:	*Little Bear,* unmarked	$12.00-15.00
	Majorette, unmarked	$15.00-18.00
	Raggedy Ann, "Japan"	$28.00-32.00

COOKIES

ROW 1:	*Sailor Monkey,* "Japan"	$15.00-18.00
	Professor Owl, "Japan"	$18.00-22.00
	Cookie Time Mouse, "Japan"	$15.00-18.00
ROW 2:	*Winking Cat,* unmarked	$18.00-22.00
	Bull Dog Police, "Japan"	$12.00-15.00
	Humpty Dumpty, "Japan"	$20.00-25.00
ROW 3:	*Granny,* unmarked	$15.00-18.00
	Mammy Biscuit Jar, unmarked	$165.00-185.00
	Rabbit, "Japan"	$15.00-18.00

COOKIES
COOKIE TIME

IF ALL ELSE FAILS ASK GRANDMA

ROW 1:	*Smiling Pear,* "6 C 30"	$15.00-18.00
	Pig on Basket, unmarked	$12.00-15.00
	Cat on Basket, unmarked	$12.00-15.00
ROW 2:	*Cookie Guard,* "Enesco Imports"	$20.00-22.00
	Raccoon Cookie Can, unmarked	$18.00-22.00
	Penguin, "Japan"	$25.00-28.00
ROW 3:	*Scarecrow,* "Royal Sealy, Japan"	$25.00-28.00
	Raggedy Ann, unmarked	$25.00-28.00
	Raggedy Andy, unmarked	$25.00-28.00

Many of the Japanese cookie jars are unmarked due to the removal of the original paper label. They are fairly easy to identify because they are not usually comparable in quality to American-made jars.

COOKIES
COOKIES
Cookie
Guard
COOKIES
CAN
COOKIES

McCoy

The Nelson McCoy Company was founded in 1910 in Roseville, Ohio. It was originally known as the Nelson McCoy Sanitary Stoneware Company. The name was changed in 1933. The plant expanded its facilities shortly thereafter and added several lines, including our beloved cookie jars from the late 1930's.

Tony Veller is the only McCoy cookie jar we know with the old Nelson McCoy mark listed in Huxford's *The Collector's Encyclopedia of McCoy Pottery.*

Who was Tony Veller? He appears to be a traveler because of his cloak and leather satchels. The bag at his feet has been tied securely and, from the load he is carrying, he has all of his worldly goods with him.

Tony Veller was designed by Sidney Cope for McCoy in the 1930's. Leslie Cope, son of Sidney Cope, feels it was a take-off on a character from Charles Dickens' *Pickwick Papers.* The character in the book is Tony Weller, which creates another mystery in cookie jar collecting: Why the "V" instead of the "W"? Was it an error or fear of copyright infringement?

A possible mate to Tony is on display at the Cope studio in Roseville, Ohio, today.

For in-depth information on McCoy Pottery, consult *The Collector's Encyclopedia of McCoy Pottery* by Sharon and Bob Huxford.

For extensive cookie jar coverage, consult *McCoy Cookie Jars, From the First to the Latest* by Harold Nichols.

TONY
Weller

ROW 1:	*Betsy Baker,* "#184, McCoy USA" (1975-76)	$70.00-75.00
	Bobby Baker, "#183, McCoy USA" (1974-1979). This jar was also re-issued from 1983-1987.	$15.00-18.00
	Betsy Baker, "#184, McCoy USA" (1975-76). There are at least three different hats for Betsy.	$70.00-75.00
ROW 2:	*Freddie the Gleep,* "#189, McCoy USA" (1974). *Freddie* is also available in green.	$70.00-75.00
	Dog House, unmarked (1983)	$48.00-52.00
	Modern Chick, unmarked (1976-1977)	$18.00-22.00
ROW 3:	*White Rooster,* #258, McCoy USA" (1970-1974)	$35.00-40.00
	Chef, "McCoy USA" (1962-1964). The *Chef* can also be found with a red scarf.	$50.00-55.00
	Hen on Basket, "USA" (1958-1959)	$38.00-42.00

COOKIES

ROW 1: *Christmas Tree,* "McCoy USA, 1959." The *Christmas Tree* is one of the most requested cookie jars by all collectors. $325.00-350.00

Santa Jar/Bank, "McCoy Limited." This jar is the real McCoy. It was produced by Nelson and Billie after the sale of the Nelson McCoy company. $115.00-125.00

Two Kittens in Low Basket, "McCoy USA" $190.00-210.00

ROW 2: *Kangaroo,* unmarked, produced after 1965 $175.00-185.00

Dalmatians, "McCoy USA, 1961" $140.00-150.00

Kangaroo, original design, "McCoy USA, 1965" $200.00-225.00

ROW 3: *Clown in Barrel,* "McCoy USA" (1953-55). The *Clown in Barrel* was also produced with yellow, blue, and green barrels. $35.00-40.00

W.C. Fields, "153, USA" (1972-74) $85.00-95.00

Hobby Horse, "McCoy USA" (1948-53) $55.00-60.00

BELOW: *Leprechaun,* unmarked. The *Leprechaun* comes in various colors. It has appeared with a green suit, red suit, and we have seen it in an all-white suit. It was originally believed that only one hundred of these jars were produced, but too many collectors have these in their possession for them to be so limited. $300.00 & up

COOKIES

ROW 1:	*Cookie Boy,* "McCoy" (1944-45)	$65.00-75.00
	Duck, unmarked (1964). The *Duck* has a leaf in his bill when turned the other way.	$50.00-55.00
	Cookie Boy, "McCoy" (1944-45)	$65.00-75.00
ROW 2:	*Penguin,* "McCoy" (1940-42)	$50.00-60.00
	Hobby Horse, "McCoy USA" (1950-51)	$58.00-62.00
	Penguin, "McCoy" (1940-43). The *Penguin* is also available in solid yellow.	$50.00-60.00
ROW 3:	*Split Trunk Elephant,* "McCoy" (1945)	$85.00-95.00
	Bear with Cookie in Vest, "McCoy" (1953). It has been rumored that this particular jar was made for the Jewell Tea Company. The colors make this a definite possibility, but, as yet, there is no proof.	$35.00-40.00
	Whole Trunk Elephant, unmarked (1953)	$65.00-75.00

Cookie Boy
Cookies
Cookies
Cookies

ROW 1:	*Bananas*, "McCoy" (1948-1952)	$55.00-60.00
	Basket of Strawberries, "McCoy USA" (1978)	$22.00-25.00
	Cookie Box or *Jewel Box*, "USA" (1963)	$50.00-55.00
ROW 2:	*Basket of Potatoes*, "0274 McCoy USA" (1978-1979)	$22.00-25.00
	Basket of Tomatoes, "0274 McCoy USA" (1978-1979)	$22.00-25.00
	Basket of Eggs, "0274 McCoy USA" (1977-1979). It's interesting that McCoy used the same base for all of these produce jars, just changing the colors and lids.	$22.00-25.00
ROW 3:	*Windmill*, "McCoy USA" (1961)	$50.00-55.00
	Kissing Penguins, "McCoy" (1946)	$42.00-45.00
	Wren House, "McCoy USA" (1960). The *Wren House* is also available with a pink bird.	$58.00-62.00

cookie box

ROW 1:	*Duck on Basketweave,* "McCoy USA" (1956)	$28.00-32.00
	Dog on Basketweave, "McCoy USA" (1956-1957)	$28.00-32.00
	Cat on Basketweave, "McCoy USA" (1956-1957)	$28.00-32.00
ROW 2:	*Pinecones on Basketweave,* "McCoy USA" (1957)	$28.00-32.00
	Apples on Basketweave, "McCoy USA" (1957)	$28.00-32.00
	Pears on Basketweave, "McCoy USA" (1957)	$28.00-32.00
ROW 3:	*Pineapple,* "McCoy USA" (1955-1957)	$30.00-35.00
	Lamb on Basketweave, "McCoy USA" (1956-1957)	$28.00-32.00
	Apple, "McCoy USA" (1950-1964). The *Apple* was also produced in yellow during this period.	$15.00-18.00

Cookies
Cookies
Cookies

Cookies
Cookies
Cookies

Cookies

ROW 1:	*Mushrooms on Stump,* "214 McCoy USA" (1972)	$18.00-22.00
	Eagle Basket, unmarked (1968-1969)	$18.00-22.00
	Monkey on Stump,"253 McCoy USA" (1970)	$20.00-25.00
ROW 2:	*Friendship 7,* unmarked (1962-1963)	$60.00-65.00
	Fortune Cookie, "McCoy USA" (1965-1968)	$28.00-32.00
	Early American Milk Can "154 USA"	$20.00-25.00
ROW 3:	*Strawberry,* "203 USA" (1972-1979)	$18.00-22.00
	Churn, unmarked (1977-1987)	$18.00-22.00
	Apple, "McCoy USA" (1970-1971)	$25.00-30.00

FRIENDSHIP
FORTUNE COOKIES
17 76
1976

COOKIE
CHURN

ROW 1:	*Rabbit on Stump*, "McCoy USA" (1971)	$28.00-32.00
	Puppy with Sign, "McCoy USA" (1961-1962)	$45.00-50.00
	Grandfather Clock, "USA" (1962-1964)	$40.00-45.00
ROW 2:	*Round Jar with Gold Trim*, "USA" (1962-1964)	$40.00-45.00
	Blue Willow Pitcher cookie jar, "202 McCoy USA" (1973-1975)	$30.00-35.00
	Tomato, "McCoy USA" (1964)	$25.00-28.00
ROW 3:	*Frontier Family*, unmarked (1964-1971)	$35.00-40.00
	Covered Wagon, "McCoy USA" (1960-1961)	$38.00-42.00
	Animal Crackers, "McCoy USA" (1960)	$25.00-28.00

COOKIE WAGON

ROW 1:	*Burlap Bag with Red Bird,* "158 USA" (1972)	$20.00-25.00
	Picnic Basket, "USA" (1961-1963)	$38.00-42.00
	Tulip, "McCoy USA" (1958-1959). The *Tulip* is also available in yellow.	$55.00-60.00
ROW 2:	*Hen on Nest,* "USA" (1958-1959)	$35.00-40.00
	Mother Goose, "McCoy USA" (1948-1952)	$60.00-65.00
	Cookie Safe, "USA" (1962-1963)	$25.00-30.00
ROW 3:	*Dutch Treat Barn,* unmarked (1968-1973)	$25.00-30.00
	Nursery Characters, *Little Bo Peep,* unmarked. The nursery characters were produced in 1970 as a set of six. The five not pictured are: *Baa Baa Black Sheep, Humpty Dumpty, Little Boy Blue, Little Miss Muffet,* and *Mary, Mary Quite Contrary.*	$18.00-22.00
	Wedding Jar, "McCoy USA" (1962)	$35.00-40.00

COOKIES

COOKIES

DUTCH TREAT
COOKIES

ROW 1:	*Cookie Barrel with Sign,* "146, McCoy USA" (1969-72)	$18.00-20.00
	Strawberry, "McCoy USA" (1955-57)	$20.00-25.00
	Pepper, "157 McCoy USA" (1972-80)	$15.00-18.00
ROW 2:	*Popeye Cylinder* (decal), unmarked (1971-72)	$40.00-45.00
	Lollipops, "McCoy USA" (1958-60)	$20.00-25.00
	Bugs Bunny Cylinder (decal), unmarked (1971-72). *Yosemite Sam* is not shown, but was produced in 1972 to complete the set of three.	$40.00-45.00
ROW 3:	*Forbidden Fruit,* "McCoy USA" (1967-68)	$18.00-22.00
	Bubbles Bank/Cookie, "224" (1985)	$28.00-32.00
	Lazy Pig, "201 McCoy USA" (1978-79)	$30.00-35.00

Cookies

COOKIES
POPEYE
COOKIES
BUGS BUNNY

ROW 1:	*Milk Can with Tree,* "277 McCoy USA" (1977)	$18.00-22.00
	Fruit Cylinder, "McCoy USA" (1946-1954)	$15.00-18.00
	Milk Can with Gingham Flowers, "333 USA"	$18.00-22.00
ROW 2:	*Pot Belly Stove,* "USA," first issued in 1963	$15.00-18.00
	Bronze Tea Kettle, "McCoy USA" (1961-67)	$18.00-22.00
	Cook Stove, "McCoy USA" (1961-69)	$18.00-22.00
ROW 3:	*Nibble Kettle,* "McCoy USA" (1960-77)	$15.00-18.00
	Cookie Jug, unmarked, first offered in 1958	$15.00-18.00
	Kookie Kettle, "McCoy USA" (1960-77)	$15.00-18.00

Cookies

Nibble
Kettle
COOKIE
JUG

ROW 1:	*Owl,* "204 McCoy USA" (1978-79)	$15.00-18.00
	Chiffonier, "McCoy USA" (1965-68)	$28.00-32.00
	Mouse, "McCoy USA" (1978-79)	$15.00-18.00
ROW 2:	*Dutch Girl,* "McCoy" (1946)	$25.00-28.00
	Dutch Boy, "McCoy" (1946)	$25.00-28.00
	Cookie Jug, "McCoy USA" (1965-68)	$15.00-18.00
ROW 3:	*Wishing Well,* "McCoy USA" (1961-70)	$18.00-22.00
	Honey Bear, "McCoy USA" (1953-55)	$28.00-32.00
	Coffee Grinder, "McCoy USA" (1961-68)	$18.00-22.00

COOKIES

Wish
I Had a
Cookie
COOKIES

ROW 1:	*Raggedy Ann,* "151 USA" (1972-75)	$40.00-50.00
	Small Clown, "McCoy" (1945)	$28.00-32.00
	Sad Clown, "255 McCoy USA" (1970-71)	$25.00-28.00
ROW 2:	*Snow Bear,* "McCoy USA" (1965)	$35.00-40.00
	Mac Dog, "208 USA" (1967-68)	$40.00-45.00
	House, "McCoy USA" (1958-60)	$48.00-52.00
ROW 3:	*Rooster,* "McCoy USA" (1956-58). The *Rooster* was produced by McCoy in two colors. The yellow as shown, and black and white.	$38.00-42.00
	Chipmunk, "McCoy USA" (1960-61)	$50.00-55.00
	Circus Horse, "McCoy USA" (1961)	$45.00-50.00

COOKIE HOUSE

ROW 1:	*Drum,* "McCoy USA" (1960)	$40.00-45.00
	Apollo, "260 McCoy, copyright USA" (1970-71)	$200.00-225.00
	Fireplace, "USA" (1967-68)	$58.00-62.00
ROW 2:	*Tug Boat,* "USA" (1985)	$15.00-18.00
	School Bus, "352 USA" (1985-86)	$15.00-20.00
	Hot-Air Balloon, "353 USA" (1985-86)	$15.00-20.00
ROW 3:	*Corn,* "275 USA" (1977)	$20.00-25.00
	Squirrel on Stump, unmarked (1965-69)	$18.00-22.00
	Kittens on Ball of Yarn, "McCoy USA" (1954-55)	$28.00-32.00

APOLLO
Bus
S.S. COOKIE
Cookie Log
Three
Little
Kittens

ROW 1:	*Concave with Rose,* "USA," mid 1930's	$15.00-18.00
	Tilt Pitcher, unmarked (1939)	$18.00-22.00
	Round Ball, unmarked (1939-44)	$15.00-18.00
ROW 2:	*Asparagus,* unmarked (1977-79)	$28.00-32.00
	Bean Pot, "USA" (1939)	$15.00-18.00
	Pear, "McCoy USA" (1956-57)	$44.00-55.00
ROW 3:	*Oaken Bucket,* unmarked (1961-71)	$18.00-22.00
	Teapot, "McCoy USA" (1972)	$28.00-32.00
	Coffee Cup, "USA" on handle (1963-66)	$28.00-32.00

ROW 1:	*Cat on Coal Bucket,* "219, McCoy USA" (1983)	$75.00-80.00
	Boy on Baseball, "221, McCoy USA" (1978)	$70.00-75.00
	Boy on Football, "222, McCoy USA" (1983). The above three cookie jars, though not very old, are already becoming highly collectible. The age of a cookie jar does not determine collectibility.	$70.00-75.00
ROW 2:	*Thinking Puppy,* "272, McCoy USA" (1977-79)	$28.00-32.00
	Hocus Rabbit, "211, McCoy USA" (1978-79)	$28.00-32.00
	Upside-down Panda, "210, McCoy USA" (1978-79)	$28.00-32.00
ROW 3:	*Happy Face,* "USA" (1972-79)	$18.00-22.00
	Happy Face Mug, unmarked	$4.00-5.00
	Happy Face Bank, unmarked	$8.00-10.00
	Happy Face Planter, unmarked	$5.00-8.00
	Timmy Tortoise, "271, McCoy USA" (1977-80)	$28.00-32.00

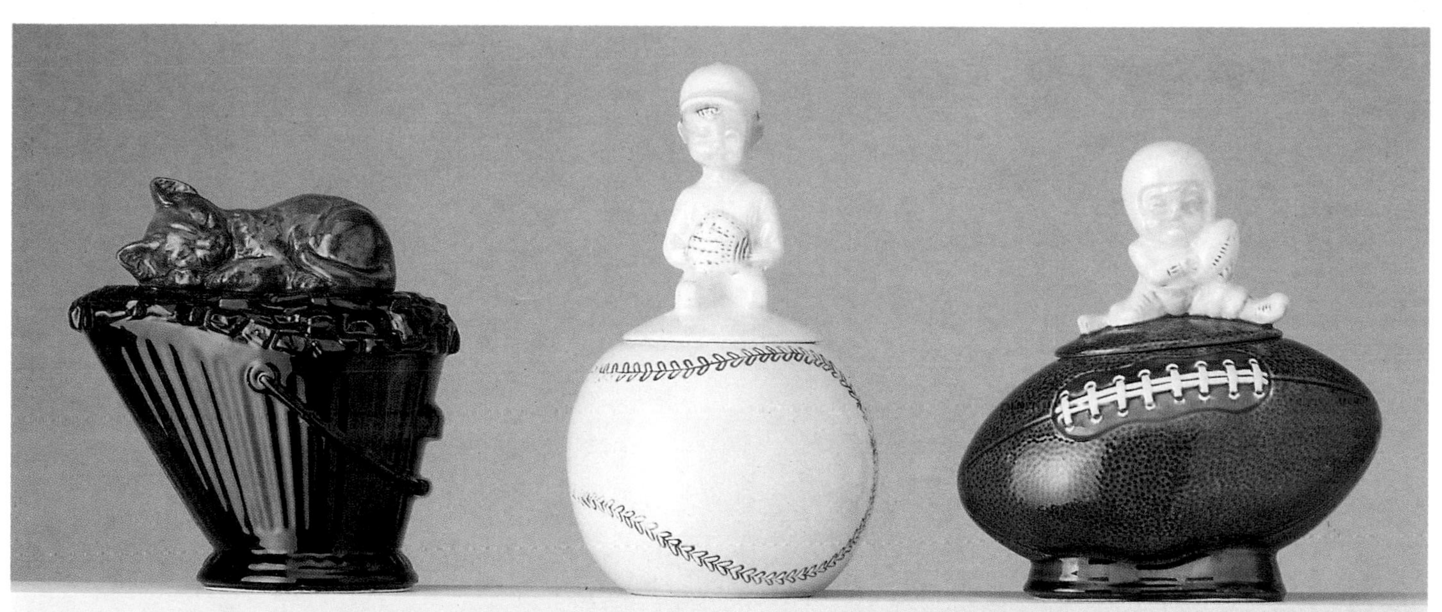

HAVE
A HAPPY DAY

ROW 1: *Indian Head,* "McCoy USA" (1954-56). The *Indian* is available in dark and light shades of brown. The lighter version is pictured here. $150.00-160.00

Tepee, "McCoy USA" (1956-59). The *Tepee* is also available with a slant, interlocking top. $150.00-160.00

Turkey, "McCoy USA" (1960). The *Turkey* is also available in white, though not as easily found as the natural colors. $115.00-125.00

ROW 2: *Davy Crockett,* "USA" (1957) $350.00-375.00

Cookie Cabin, "McCoy USA" (1956-60) $40.00-45.00

Mr. and Mrs. Owl, "McCoy USA" (1952-55) $55.00-60.00

ROW 3: *Coalby Cat,* "USA" $115.00-125.00

Jack-O'-Lantern, "McCoy USA" (1955). The *Jack-O-Lantern* is also available with an orange lid. $240.00-250.00

Corn, "McCoy USA" 1958-59 $90.00-95.00

Many of the jars pictured on this page make fantastic holiday decorations and table centerpieces. Take advantage of this and enjoy your cookie jars.

BELOW: *Fox Squirrel,* "McCoy" (1961) $250.00-275.00

Cookies
COOKIE CABIN
Davy Crockett
COOKIES

ROW 1:	*Touring Car,* "McCoy USA" (1962-64)	$55.00-60.00
	World Globe, "McCoy USA" (1960)	$90.00-95.00
	Cookie Bank/Jar, McCoy USA" (1961)	$70.00-75.00
ROW 2:	*Granite Coffee Pot,* unmarked (1974-75)	$50.00-60.00
	Tea Kettle, "McCoy USA" (1961-67)	$22.00-28.00
	Cookie Coffee Pot, "McCoy USA" (1964-74)	$25.00-30.00
ROW 3:	*Barn,* "McCoy USA" (1963)	$130.00-150.00
	Cookie Barrel, unmarked (1958-68)	$18.00-22.00
	Cookie Boy, "McCoy" (1944-45)	$65.00-75.00

Cookie Bank

cookie pot

Cookies

ROW 1: *Engine,* "McCoy USA" (1962-64) $100.00-125.00

Caboose, "McCoy USA" (1961) $100.00-125.00

Engine, "McCoy USA" (1962-64) $100.00-125.00

Though the yellow and pumpkin-colored engines are not found as frequently as the black, the realism of the traditional engine helps it hold its value.

ROW 2: *Winking Pig,* "#150, USA" (1972) $80.00-90.00

Engine, "McCoy USA" (1962-64) $100.00-125.00

Grandma, "USA" (1972-73). *Grandma* was also produced in 1974-75 wearing a white dress and gold wire-rimmed glasses. $45.00-50.00

ROW 3: *Woodsy Owl,* "USA" (1973-74) $85.00-95.00

Monk, unmarked (1968-73) $28.00-32.00

Snoopy on Dog House, "USA" (1970). *Snoopy* is also marked with a stamp, "United Features Syndicate, Inc., World Rights Reserved." Made in USA for Sears, Roebuck and Company. $115.00-125.00

COOKIE
COOKIE SPECIAL
COOKIE

DON'T POLLUTE
WOODSY OWL
SNOOPY

ROW 1:	*Dogs on Cylinder,* "McCoy USA"	$65.00-75.00
	Stagecoach, unmarked	$300.00 & up
	Cat on Cylinder, "McCoy USA"	$65.00-75.00
ROW 2:	*Chilly Willy,* "155 USA" (1986-1989)	$30.00-35.00
	Chairman of the Board, "162 USA" (1985)	$85.00-95.00
	Kitten on Coal Bucket, "218 USA" (1983)	$115.00-125.00
ROW 3:	*Kids' Stuff Cat,* "1502 USA" (1989)	$20.00-25.00
	Kids' Stuff Dog, "1501 USA" (1989)	$20.00-25.00
	Little Jack Horner, unmarked. This jar possibly is by McCoy. It is heavy and appears old, but there is no positive identification.	$200.00 & up

When a pottery produces a jar for one year, like the *Chairman of the Board* and the *Kitten on Coal Bucket,* the price mirrors the demand.

Metlox Potteries

The Metlox Pottery Company was founded in Manhattan Beach, California, in 1927. In 1947, the plant was purchased by Evan K. Shaw and the production of cookie jars began.

Metlox also produced cookie jars under the trade name "Poppy Trail of California," which is a division of Metlox.

Though Evan Shaw died in 1980, the company remained in the Shaw family under the management of Ken Avery, son-in-law of Evan Shaw. The outstanding quality product continued until June 1, 1989, when the doors were closed on this family enterprise which lasted nearly half a century.

ROW 1:	*Clown,* "Made in Poppytrail, Calif."	$40.00-45.00
	Clown, "Met" unconfirmed Metlox	$30.00-35.00
	Clown, "Made in Poppytrail, Calif."	$40.00-45.00
ROW 2:	*Beaver,* unmarked	$38.00-42.00
	Frog, unmarked	$38.00-42.00
	Squirrel on Pinecone, "Made in USA"	$30.00-35.00
ROW 3:	*Owl,* unmarked	$28.00-32.00
	Sir Francis Drake, unmarked	$38.00-42.00
	Panda Bear, unmarked	$30.00-35.00

ROW 1:	*Pinocchio,* paper label: "Made in Calif., Poppytrail Pottery by Metlox"	$70.00-80.00
	Rabbit on Cabbage, unmarked	$30.00-35.00
	Little Red Riding Hood, "Made in Poppytrail, Calif."	$100.00-125.00
ROW 2:	*Raggedy Andy,* "Made in Poppytrail, Calif."	$40.00-45.00
	Cub Scout, unmarked	$65.00-75.00
	Raggedy Ann, "Made in Poppytrail, Calif."	$40.00-45.00
ROW 3:	*Cat,* unmarked, not Melox but Gustin of Los Angeles Pottery	$30.00-35.00
	Drum, bisque, "Made in Poppytrail, Calif."	$30.00-35.00
	Cat, unmarked, not Metlox but Gustin of Los Angeles	$30.00-35.00

ROW 1:	*Baby Bluebird on Pinecone,* "Made in USA," paper label: "Metlox Manufacturing Co."	$45.00-50.00
	Brownie Scout, paper label: "Metlox Manufacturing Co.," also paper label: "Made in California, Poppytrail Pottery by Metlox"	$90.00-100.00
	Downey Woodpecker, "Made in Poppytrail, Calif. USA"	$45.00-50.00
ROW 2:	*Dino,* "Metlox Calif. USA copyright '87 by Vincent"	$65.00-75.00
	Mona, "Metlox Calif. USA copyright '87 by Vincent"	$65.00-75.00
	Rex, "Metlox Calif. USA copyright '87 by Vincent"	$65.00-75.00
ROW 3:	*Barn,* "Metlox Calif. USA"	$55.00-60.00
	Cat, "Metlox Calif. USA"	$55.00-60.00
	Dog, "Metlox Calif. USA"	$45.00-50.00
BELOW:	*Mrs. Rabbit,* "Metlox Calif. USA"	$55.00-60.00
	Pelican, "US Diving Team," "Metlox Calif. USA"	$55.00-60.00
	Bisque Piggy, "Made in Poppytrail, Calif. USA"	$45.00-50.00
	Slenderella, "Metlox Calif. USA."	$55.00-60.00

Pages 164 thru 169 are catalog reprints of Metlox.

617
655
656
613
612
611
614
632
623
620
619
616
615

193 550
194 550
192 550

550 cookie jars
POPPYTRAIL ARTWARE
196 550 Clown, White
200 550 Teddy Bear
202 550 Little Red Riding Hood
197 550 Pretty Ann
195 550 Grapefruit
198 550 Cow with Butterfly, Yellow
201 550 Ginger Bread
203 550 Green with Daisy Lid
204 550 Yellow with Daisy Lid

New for 1978
POPPYTRAIL ARTWARE
HAND-DECORATED COOKIE JARS
METLOX POTTERIES • MANHATTAN BEACH, CA 90266
1.
2.
3.
4.
5.
6.
7.
8.
9.
1. 561 550 Cookie Bandit - W $24.95
2. 568 550 Teddy Bear - W $24.95
3. 563 550 Owls on Stump - W $24.95
4. 559 550 Gingerbread - W $76.95
5. 569 550 Mouse Mobile - W $26.95
6. 564 550 Cookie Girl - W $24.95
7. 566 650 Bubbles $24.95
8. 562 550 Noah's Ark - W $24.95
9. 560 550 Little Piggy - W $24.95

CHICKEN (MOTHER HEN)
CALF (FERDINAND)
CAT, CALICO
DOG, FIDO
DOG, BASSETT
BEAR, BALLERINA
BEAR, BEAU
BEAR, KOALA
BEAR, PANDA
BEAR, ROLLER
BEAR, SOMBRERO (PANCHO)
BEAR, TEDDY, BROWN
SEAL (SAMMY)
MOUSE, CHEF (PIERRE)
CLOWN, WHITE
CAT, KATY
PENGUIN (FROSTY)
DOG, SCOTTIE (WHITE)
DOG, SCOTTIE (BLACK)

APPLE
BEAR, BEAU
BEAR, PANDA
BEAR, SOMBRERO (PANCHO)
BEAR, TEDDY, BROWN
CAT, ALI
CAT, KATY
CLOWN, WHITE
DOG, SCOTTIE (BLACK)
DOG, SCOTTIE (WHITE)
DUCK (PUDDLES)
DUCK, FRANCINE
DUCK (SIR FRANCIS DRAKE)
GOOSE, LUCY
HUMPTY DUMPTY
LAMB, WHITE
MAMMY (COOK)
Julius Cheeser
MOUSE, CHEF (PIERRE)
PENGUIN (FROSTY)

DUCK BLUES
DUCK, (SIR FRANCIS DRAKE)
GOOSE, LUCY
DUCK (PUDDLES)
APPLE
ORANGE
STRAWBERRY
PUMPKIN
RABBIT ON CABBAGE
RACCOON (COOKIE BANDIT)
RABBIT
PIG, LITTLE
PIG, SLENDERELLA
LAMB, WHITE
HUMPTY DUMPTY
RABBIT (MRS. BUNNY)

NEW
NEW
PIG, LITTLE
PIG, SLENDERELLA
RABBIT, EASTER BUNNY
RABBIT, MRS. BUNNY
RABBIT ON CABBAGE
STRAWBERRY
DUTCH BOY
DUTCH GIRL
NEW
NEW
NEW
BLUE BIRD
LADY'S BONNET CHIP 'N DIP
COW BANK
RABBIT BANK
PIGGY BANK (IRA)
CABBAGE CHIP 'N DIP
BBQ Plate 11"
Demitasse
Cup & Saucer
5 oz.
Buffet Plate 12"
Jumbo
Cup & Saucer
16 oz.
Coupe Plate 13"
CHRISTMAS
SHELL CHIP 'N DIP, LOTUS COLORS
COLORSTAX COLORS

Cookie Jars from
Poppytrail
636
642
622
639
628
614
627
621
618
624
625
623
655
656
630
634
615
611
617
612
616
620
619
613
663
METLOX POTTERIES
Distributed by EVAN K. SHAW CO., 527 W. 7th St., Los Angeles, Calif.

Miscellaneous

The American Pottery Company was founded as the Stoin-Lee Pottery Company and, originally, was located in Byesville, Ohio. In 1942, the company name was changed and the offices were moved to Marietta, Ohio.

J.B. Lenhart and A.N. Allen were joint owners of APCO prior to 1944 when Allen sold his interest to Lenhart and concentrated his efforts on American Bisque in Williamstown, West Virginia.

Lenhart continued the American Pottery operation until 1961 when he sold to R.J. Braden. Braden served on the Board of Directors and appointed John Bonistall, former president of Shawnee, as president and general manager.

J.B. Lenhart also worked for A.N. Allen at American Bisque when he owned APCO, which tied the two companies so closely together that many similarities in their designs are apparent. Also, many of the identifying mold marks are so worn that it is very hard to decipher between "APCO" and "ABCO."

The American Pottery Company was closed in 1965.

ROW 1:	*Clown with "U's" on Collar,* "USA, APCO"	$20.00-25.00
	Clown, American Bisque, "USA 126A"	$35.00-38.00
	Clown with Stripes on Collar, "USA, APCO"	$20.00-25.00
ROW 2:	*Dutch Boy,* "USA APCO"	$28.00-32.00
	Bear, "USA APCO"	$20.00-25.00
	Dutch Girl, "USA, APCO"	$28.00-32.00
ROW 3:	*Pig in Overalls,* "USA, APCO"	$18.00-22.00
	Lamb in Overalls, "USA, APCO"	$18.00-22.00
	Cow in Overalls, "USA, APCO"	$18.00-22.00

ROW 1:	*Rabbit in Basket,* "Patent Pending," recently identified as early American Bisque	$30.00-35.00
	Cat in Basket, "Patent Pending," also American Bisque	$30.00-35.00
	Dog in Basket, "Patent Pending," American Bisque	$30.00-35.00
ROW 2:	*Chef,* unmarked, also salt and pepper available	$18.00-22.00
	Pig Dancer, unmarked American Bisque	$38.00-42.00
	Salt and Pepper to match *Pig Dancer,* unmarked	$12.00-15.00
	Pig Dancer, unmarked, American Bisque	$38.00-42.00
ROW 3:	*Elephant,* "USA," manufactured by Ludowici Celadon	$28.00-32.00
	Belmont Lion, "Belmont" written in script, produced by Ludowici Celadon for an unknown client	$20.00-25.00
	Helmet, unmarked	$30.00-35.00
	Boy/Girl Bear Turnabout, "Patent Applied Turnabout, The 4-1," manufactured by Ludowici Celadon	$35.00-40.00
BELOW:	*Sweet Notes,* unmarked	$50.00-60.00
	Miss Muffet, "5749"	$100.00-125.00
	Policeman, unmarked	$50.00-55.00

ABCO & APCO

ROW 1:	*Polka Dot Kitty,* "Pat. Design ABCO 131 USA"	$38.00-42.00
	Miniature Bear, "APCO Pat. Design"	$35.00-38.00
	Clown with Patches, "APCO Pat. Design"	$20.00-25.00

Brazil

ROW 2:	*Tiger,* "Made in Brazil"	$15.00-18.00
	Elephant, "Made in Brazil"	$15.00-18.00

American Greetings

Tenderheart Bear, "Tenderheart Bear - One of the Care Bears copyright MCMLXXXIV American Greetings Corp., Cleveland, Ohio 44144 Made in Korea 53044"	$35.00-45.00
Funshine Bear, "Funshine Bear - One of the Care Bears, copyright MCMLXXXIV American Greetings Corp., Cleveland, Ohio. Made in Korea 53044"	$35.00-45.00

Brayton Laguna

ROW 3:	*Dog,* unmarked	$75.00-85.00
	Circus Tent, stamped "Brayton Laguna"	$60.00-70.00
	Clown and Dog salt and pepper, *Clown* stamped "Brayton"	$25.00-30.00
	Lady, "Brayton Laguna"	$100.00-130.00
BELOW:	*Granny,* "Brayton Laguna, Calif. 40-85"	$115.00-130.00
	Girl and Boy salt and pepper shakers	$40.00-50.00
	Goose Woman, "Brayton Laguna Pottery"	$135.00-145.00

Brayton

BELOW: *Gypsy Lady,* unmarked $110.00-120.00

Swedish Maiden, "Brayton Laguna Pottery copyright" $115.00-125.00

DeForest of California

DeForest is yet another family-owned California enterprise. Originally begun as a hobby of Margaret DeForest in 1950, the business grew until a corporation was formed. Her husband Jack DeForest served as president, and their sons played an important role in the further growth and development of the company.

DeForest remained in business until 1970 when many circumstances forced their demise.

ROW 1: *Rabbit in Hat,* "DeForest of Calif., copyright, USA" $28.00-32.00

Mrs. Rabbit, "DeForest of Calif." $28.00-32.00

Clown, "Deforest of Calif., copyright USA" $20.00-25.00

ROW 2: *Little King,* "DeForest of Calif., copyright 1957" $45.00-50.00

Holiday Designs

Holiday Designs is located in Sebring, Ohio, in the building previously occupied by Spaulding China Company. The business was incorporated in 1964.

Today, Holiday Designs is part of a large conglomerate called Designer Accents which was established in early 1986.

ROW 2: *Snoopy,* not copyrighted, "Holiday Designs" $35.00-40.00

ROW 3: *Happy Face,* unmarked $30.00-35.00

Elf, "Holiday Designs" $28.00-32.00

Pumpkin, "Holiday Designs" $28.00-32.00

KOOKIE
KLOWN
Cookie
King!

Lane

The only information we can find on Lane is from the marks on the jars themselves and a paper label affixed to one.

A large clock, not pictured, has a paper label stating "Distinctive American Craftsmanship For Over Twenty-Five Years."

ROW 1: *Indian,* "copyright, 1950 Lane and Co., Los Angeles, Calif.," artist signed, "R. Nickerson" $250.00-275.00

Clown, "Lane and Co. Los Angeles, copyright, 1950" $50.00-55.00

Sheriff, "copyright 1950, Lane and Co., Los Angeles" $150.00-160.00

Maddux of California

The Maddux Pottery was established in Los Angeles, California, by William Maddux. In 1948, William Maddux sold the company to Louis and Dave Warsaw. During the 1950's when many of the pottery companies were floundering due to Japanese imports, Maddux was also having its share of problems.

Dave Warsaw sold his share of Maddux to Morris Bogdanow in 1956. Bogdanow eventually bought the remaining shares to become sole owner. It was during this transition period that Maddux began producing cookie jars.

The total operation ceased in 1980.

ROW 2: *Raggedy Andy,* "copyright, Maddux of Calif. USA 2108" $38.00-42.00

Humpty Dumpty, "2113 copyright, Maddux of Calif. USA" $38.00-42.00

ROW 3: *Beatrix Potter Rabbit,* "copyright, Maddux of Calif." $60.00-70.00

Cat, "copyright, Maddux of Calif." $60.00-70.00

Raggedy Andy and *Beatrix Potter Rabbit* are not copyrighted as such; they just seem to fit the appearance of the characters.

BELOW: *Bear,* "Maddux of Calif. copyright USA 2101" $50.00-60.00

Squirrel Hiker, "Maddux of Calif. copyright Romanell 2110" $48.00-52.00

Maurice of California

Very little is known about Maurice other than it was a commercial enterprise located in Los Angeles, California.

After checking with Directory Assistance in Los Angeles, Joyce found there is no longer a telephone listing for Maurice, but the possibility remains that they may have relocated.

ROW 1: *Gigantic Clown,* "Maurice of Calif. USA JA 10" $35.00-38.00

Sitting Bear, "Maurice of Calif. USA" $24.00-30.00

Train, "Maurice of Calif. USA JD 45" $28.00-32.00

ROW 2: *Elephant,* "Maurice of Calif. USA 1976, PG-61 Ceramic." $22.00-25.00

Puzzled Monkey, "Maurice of Calif. USA" $35.00-40.00

Chef, also gigantic, "Maurice of Calif." $42.00-48.00

ROW 3: *Love Me Dog,* "Maurice of Calif. USA" $28.00-32.00

Hobo Clown, "Made in Mexico" $18.00-22.00

Leopard, "Made in Mexico" $18.00-22.00

BELOW: *Noah's Ark,* "Pat. Pending Starnes, Calif." $65.00-75.00

Dog on Drum, "Sierra Vista, California" $45.00-50.00

COOKIE

LOVE ME

Morton Pottery Company

The Morton Pottery Company was opened in Morton, Illinois, by the Rapp brothers in 1922. The first cookie jar the pottery produced was the *Hen with Chick Finial* in 1930, which remained in production until the 1950's.

The pottery continued with the Rapp family at its helm until 1969 when it was sold, but operations continued under the Morton name until 1971 when financial difficulties forced its closing.

ROW 1:	*Fruit Basket,* "USA 3720"	$25.00-30.00
	Coffee Pot, "USA 3721"	$18.00-22.00
	Milk Can, "USA 3539"	$20.00-25.00
ROW 2:	*Hen with Chick,* unmarked	$30.00-35.00
	Ozark Hillbilly, unmarked	$30.00-35.00
	Turkey, unmarked	$50.00-60.00

Napco, Japanese

ROW 3:	*Spaceship,* "Napco"	$20.00-25.00
	Pixie, "Napco"	$18.00-22.00
	Betsy Ross, label, "Imports, Enesco, Japan"	$20.00-25.00
	Red Riding Hood, "Napco"	$50.00-60.00
	Cinderella, "J.C. Napco 1957 K2292"	$50.00-60.00

COOKIES
OUT OF THIS WORLD!

"Out to Pasture"

ROW 1:	*Daisy Cow,* "copyright OCI" (Omnibus)	$55.00-65.00
	Quilted Cow, unmarked	$25.00-30.00
	Patchwork Cow, unmarked	$25.00-30.00
ROW 2:	*Holstein Cow,* "copyright Otagiri"	$60.00-65.00
	Cow Beach Woody, "copyright Vandor 1988." "MOO-1" on license	$35.00-40.00
	Cow Beach salt and pepper, marked exactly like the cookie jar	$12.00-15.00
	McCoy Cow, "8166 USA." This jar is not dishwasher safe, the spots come off.	$45.00-55.00
ROW 3:	*Winton Cow,* "copyright Alberta's Molds Inc. 1981." Don Winton sculpted this mold for the Alberta Mold Company.	$40.00-45.00
	Cow with Milk Carton, unmarked	$25.00-35.00
	Softie Cow, "CKJ2 copyright 1987 NAC USA." The enclosed card states "Hand decorated by Julia." NAC is North American Ceramics, Inc. of Los Angeles, California. The company no longer produces cookie jars.	$40.00-45.00
BELOW:	*Continental Cow,* paper label: "Made in Portugal Over and Back Inc." Note her glass eyes.	$36.00-42.00
	Cowmen Mooranda, "copyright Vandor 1988." Salt and pepper sets are also available for *Cowmen.*	$35.00-40.00
	Wang Cow, unmarked	$18.00-22.00

MILK

Pan American Art

Pan American Art is a known mark of the San Jose Potteries, which was located in San Antonio, Texas, during the middle 1940's.

ROW 1: Cinderella-type *Lady*, "Pan American Art" $18.00-22.00

Clown, "Pan American Art" $18.00-22.00

Pearl China, See Black Americana

ROW 2: *Bear* with heavy, heavy gold. "Pearl, in shell, China Co. Hand Decorated 22 Kt. Gold U.S.A." $85.00-95.00

Bear, as above, same marks $90.00-100.00

Pitman-Dreitzer and Company

The popular *Fruit Kids* were distributed by the Pitman-Dreitzer Company, a New York selling agency. The actual manufacturer remains a mystery for now.

ROW 3: *Albert Apple*, "FKR 1942 P D & Co., Inc.," signed "Albert Apple" $50.00-60.00

The following *Fruit Kids* Chalk Figurines are available from the same era.

Albert Apple, "copyright 1942 Pee Dee" $12.00-15.00

Stella Strawberry, "copyright 1942 Pee Dee" $12.00-15.00

Priscilla Pineapple, "copyright 1942 Pee Dee" $12.00-15.00

Charlie Cherry, "copyright 1942 Pee Dee" $12.00-15.00

Lee Lemon, "copyright 1942 Pee Dee" $12.00-15.00

Stella Strawberry, "FKR 1942 P D & Co., Inc.," signed "Stella Strawberry" $60.00-65.00

Pfaltzgraff Pottery Company

The Pfaltzgraff Pottery Company was founded in 1811 by a German immigrant, George Pfaltzgraff, in York, Pennsylvania.

Pfaltzgraff is unique inasmuch as it is a family-owned pottery still operated by the descendants of the original founder.

At present, the only cookie jars produced by Pfaltzgraff are non-figurals matching their dinnerware.

ROW 1: *Derby Dan,* "Derby Dan, Muggsie, The Pfaltzgraff Pottery Co., York, Penn. Designed by Jessop" $45.00-50.00

Cockeye Charlie, "Cockeye Charlie, Muggsie, The Pfaltzgraff Co., York, Penn. Designed by Jessop" $18.00-22.00

Jerry the Jerk, "Jerry the Jerk, Muggsie, The Pfaltzgraff Co., York, Penn. Designed by Jessop" $18.00-22.00

Clock, unmarked $28.00-32.00

Flirty Gertie, "Flirty Gertie, Muggsie, The Pfaltzgraff Co., York, Penn. Designed by Jessop" $18.00-22.00

Train, unmarked $40.00-45.00

ROW 2: *Cooky girl,* unmarked, unknown $22.00-28.00

Hobby Horse, "602," paper label: "Pidgeon Vitrified China Co., Barnhart, Mo. USA." This is from the Abingdon mold. Pidgeon purchased part of these molds. $40.00-45.00

Miss Muffet, unmarked, Abingdon copy, but not from the original mold. In addition to the dry foot, there is a small, filled, unglazed circle in the center of the bottom. $38.00-42.00

ROW 3: *Train,* "681," artist signed, "K.S." This jar is also from the original Abingdon mold, but this time there is no label to aid in identification. $45.00-50.00

Roseville Cylinder, "R 20 USA" $50.00-60.00

Roseville Clematis, "USA 3 - 8" $150.00-160.00

COOKIE TIME

"COOKY"

ROW 1: *Pirate on Chest,* "Pat. Pending, Starnes of Calif., copyright" $75.00-80.00

Terrace Ceramics

The Terrace Ceramics Company of Marietta, Ohio, was founded by John Bonistall, president of Shawnee, after Shawnee's liquidation. Bonistall purchased part of the Shawnee molds and made products with the Terrace Ceramic mark. The plant closed in 1974.

Corn, "Terrace Ceramics, USA, 4299" $50.00-55.00

Bear, "Terrace Ceramics, USA" $20.00-25.00

ROW 2: *Mugsey,* "Mugsey, Terrace Ceramics, USA" $50.00-55.00

Cat, "Terrace Ceramics USA 4253" $35.00-40.00

ROW 3: *Rabbit,* "Terrace Ceramics USA 4254." Apparently Bonistall also purchased some APCO molds. $30.00-35.00

Peter Pumpkin Eater, "Vallona Starr Design Pat. copyright 49 California" $60.00-70.00

Vallona Starr is a part of Triangle Studios, El Monte,California, which operated during the 1950's.

BELOW: *Raggedy Ann,* "Pat. Applied For," unknown $50.00-60.00

Raggedy Ann Bank, unmarked $28.00-32.00

Raggedy Ann salt and pepper, unmarked $15.00-18.00

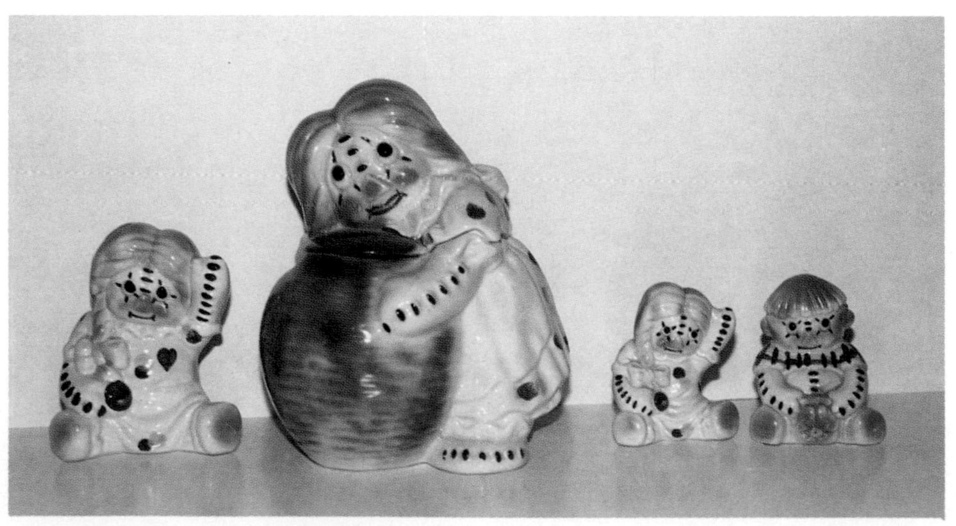

Christmas

ROW 1: *Standing Santa,* "Metlox Calif. USA" $50.00-60.00

Boot of Toys, unmarked, also available in terra cotta $30.00-35.00

ROW 2: *Snowman,* "copyright FF." $55.00-65.00

Mrs. Claus, "copyright F.F. Japan" $75.00-85.00

Panda, "Fitz and Floyd, Inc. copyright MCMLXXXIV, FF" $50.00-55.00

ROW 3: *Uncle Mistletoe,* "Uncle Mistletoe Cookie Jar, Pat. copyright 50028," produced by Regal China for Marshall Field. A similar mold design was used by Peter Pan Products Inc., Chicago, Illinois. The main difference between the two is the cold paint used on the coat and face of the Peter Pan, and the fired gold on the Regal. The Regal hat looks the same but is actually smaller than the Peter Pan. $175.00-185.00

Art Deco Santa, "N.S. Gustin Co., Hand Decorated. Made in U.S.A." $50.00-60.00

Glass Bowl Santa, "Treasure Craft, copyright Made in USA." $75.00-80.00

ROW 1:	*Combination Snowman,* "Riddell copyright" The teapot on top, the cookie jar is the base.	$90.00-100.00
	Santa with Toy Bag, "copyright Alberta's Molds Inc. 1980"	$40.00-45.00
	Snowman and Glass, "copyright Treasure Craft, Made in USA"	$50.00-60.00
ROW 2:	*Santa,* "Made in Brazil." This jar was featured in K-Mart"s Christmas in July, 1988.	$25.00-28.00
	Snowman, "Made in Mexico" on paper label	$30.00-35.00
	Musical Santa, unmarked	$38.00-42.00
ROW 3:	*Paddington Bear,* "Paddington by Toscany, copyright Eden 1987"	$40.00-45.00
	Two-story House, unmarked. This is actually a three-piece jar.	$30.00-35.00
	Gingerbread House, "Treasure Craft Compton, California Made in U.S.A." on paper label	$30.00-35.00
BELOW:	*Mrs. Santa,* "copyright 1987 Houston Foods" on the original box	$18.00-22.00
	Mr. Santa, "copyright 1987 Houston Foods" on the original box	$18.00-22.00
	Rocking Chair Santa, "54-193 House of Lloyd for Christmas Around the World," on the original box	$18.00-22.00

ROW 1:	*Goose,* "Made in Mexico" on paper label	$30.00-35.00
	Tree, unmarked	$30.00-35.00
	Goose, unmarked, Treasure Craft	$35.00-40.00
ROW 2:	*Santa,* unmarked	$30.00-35.00
	Christmas Cow, unmarked	$50.00-60.00
	Dog in Boot, "Made in Mexico" on paper label	$30.00-35.00
ROW 3:	*Santa Head,* "Mallory copyright Inc."	$38.00-42.00
	Santa at Desk, unmarked Alberta mold	$50.00-60.00
	Santa Head, "Metlox Calif. USA," paper label: "Wash me carefully-Thanks, Santa, Metlox Calif. U.S.A."	$40.00-50.00
BELOW:	*Winton Santa,* marked on inside rim of lid: "An Original Sculpture by Don Winton"	$38.00-42.00

ACCOUNTING DEPT.
S.CLAUS MGR.

ROW 1: *Santa,* plastic, unmarked $30.00-35.00

Santa in Easy Chair, unmarked $60.00-70.00

Santa, plastic, "Made in USA, copyright Carolina Enterprises Inc., Tarboro, N.C. 1973" $30.00-35.00

ROW 2: *Small Standing Santa,* silver label illegible $28.00-32.00

Winking Santa, unmarked, Lefton China $38.00-42.00

Musical Santa, unmarked, plays "Jingle Bells" $45.00-50.00

Enesco Santa, "copyright, 1980 Enesco" $40.00-45.00

ROW 3: *Santa,* unmarked, excellent quality older jar $50.00-60.00

Santa, unmarked, cold paint. Notice how this jar sits on runners or bars just as a few of the McCoy jars do. $50.00-60.00

ABC Santa, "USA" $115.00-125.00

COOKIES

ROW 1: *Glass Bowl Pig,* "Treasure Craft, copyright. Made in USA" $45.00-55.00

Pig or *Alien?* "copyright 1968 Pacific Stoneware Inc. USA Joll Flower," artist signed "Scarpino" $30.00-35.00

Shaggy Dog Head, unmarked $35.00-40.00

ROW 2: *Cadillac,* unmarked, but made by North American Ceramics $50.00-55.00

1956 Porsche, "ACCJ2 copyright 1986," North American Ceramics $50.00-55.00

Van, "843 USA," by California Originals $40.00-45.00

ROW 3: *1950 Jaguar,* "ACCJ 5 copyright 1986 NAC USA" $50.00-60.00

Transformer, "Manufactured by: Great American Housewares Inc. New York - N.Y. 10003 copyright Hasbro Bradley Inc. All rights reserved. Made in Portugal" $70.00-75.00

1957 Chevrolet, "Made in Portugal" $45.00-50.00

TRANS FORMERS

ROW 1:	*Designosaur,* unmarked	$35.00-40.00
	Lady Dragon, unmarked	$20.00-25.00
	Dinosaur, by Dino-Store, unmarked	$20.00-25.00
ROW 2:	*Ricky Raccoon,* The Shirttales Cookie Jar, "Made in Taiwan, copyright, 1981 Hallmark Cards Inc."	$35.00-40.00
	Juke Box, Auxilary wall box, by Vandor	$60.00-70.00
	Monkey in Barrel, "CJ 43 USA." This is probably Doranne.	$38.00-42.00
ROW 3:	*Mouse,* "J 53 Calif. USA," Doranne of California	$38.00-42.00
	Spuds, "Taiwan"	$28.00-32.00
	Entenmann's Chef, "B & D copyright." Originally this chef came complete with the bakery decal on the hat which was not dishwasher proof. Joyce knew the scarf had cold paint, but never gave a thought to the decal until she opened the dishwasher and found it resting on his eye.	$40.00-45.00

Cookie Bandit
COOKIES
1234567
MR. COOKIE
GOURMET

Row 1: *Gorilla with Lady in Hand* (King Kong ???), "Omnibus 1987" $65.00-75.00

Miss Piggy, unmarked $28.00-32.00

Emmett Kelly Jr., "The Emmett Kelly Jr. Collection Exclusively from Flambro" $95.00-105.00

ROW 2: *Betty Boop*, "copyright 1985 King Features Syndicate, Inc." $150.00-175.00

Howdy Doody, paper label: "Vandor, Made in Japan" $65.00-75.00

Howdy Doody Bumper Car, "1988 Vandor copyright" $38.00-42.00

Howdy Doody in Car salt and pepper, paper label: "Vandor Made in Japan." The salt and pepper actually belong with the *Howdy Doody* cookie jar. $12.00-15.00

ROW 3: *Big Bird*, "copyright MUPPETS INC.," NEWCOR USA $28.00-32.00

Ernie, "copyright MUPPETS INC.," distributed by NEWCOR USA $28.00-32.00

Cookie Monster, "copyright MUPPETS INC.," NEWCOR USA $28.00-32.00

COOKIES
COOKIES

ROW 1: *Girl with Crown,* unmarked $70.00-80.00

Cinderella, unmarked. There is also a *Red Riding Hood* from the identical mold which was cold-painted. $65.00-75.00

Boy with Crown, unmarked $70.00-80.00

ROW 2: *Family Circus' Billy,* unmarked. Let the debate begin! We felt there was a strong resemblance to "Dennis the Menace" until we found the matching little girl. Dennis' little girlfriend was Margaret, who had red hair and wore glasses. Since these jars are neither marked nor copyrighted, call them what you wish. $65.00-75.00

Debutante, "82" on bottom, paper label inside lid, "T.M. James and Sons China Co., Kansas City, Missouri." The Stetson China Company produced jars for the T.M. James and Sons China Company, but it is unknown who actually produced this particular jar. $65.00-75.00

Family Circus' Dolly, unmarked $65.00-75.00

ROW 3: *Dutch Boy,* unmarked, gold-trimmed $85.00-95.00

Indian Lady, unmarked. This cookie jar was not produced by American Bisque according to A.N. Allen, former owner of American Bisque. $55.00-65.00

Dutch Girl, unmarked, gold-trimmed. The *Dutch Girl* and *Dutch Boy* are possibly early American Bisque, since they appear to be from the "ABC" mold. We know American Bisque did gold firing, but have never seen one with decals similar to Shawnee's decorated jars. $85.00-95.00

Cookies
Cookies

ROW 1:	*Telephone,* unmarked	$35.00-40.00
	Doranne of California *Lunch Box,* unmarked	$28.00-32.00
	Doranne of California *Mail Box,* unmarked	$35.00-40.00
ROW 2:	*Tuggles,* unmarked. There are at least three versions of *Tuggles.* Starnes produced one using a paper label, one is totally unmarked, and one is marked "California."	$60.00-70.00
	Howdy Doody, unmarked, Purinton	$200.00-225.00
	Cool Cat, unmarked, excellent quality	$75.00-85.00
ROW 3:	*Rocking Horse,* unmarked	$38.00-42.00
	Neal the Frog, unmarked. Sears sold this jar approximately five years ago, under the trade name "Freddie Frog."	$25.00-30.00
	Carrousel, "USA"	$18.00-22.00
BELOW:	*White Stagecoach,* unmarked, possibly McCoy	$200.00-225.00

U.S. MAIL
U.S. MAIL

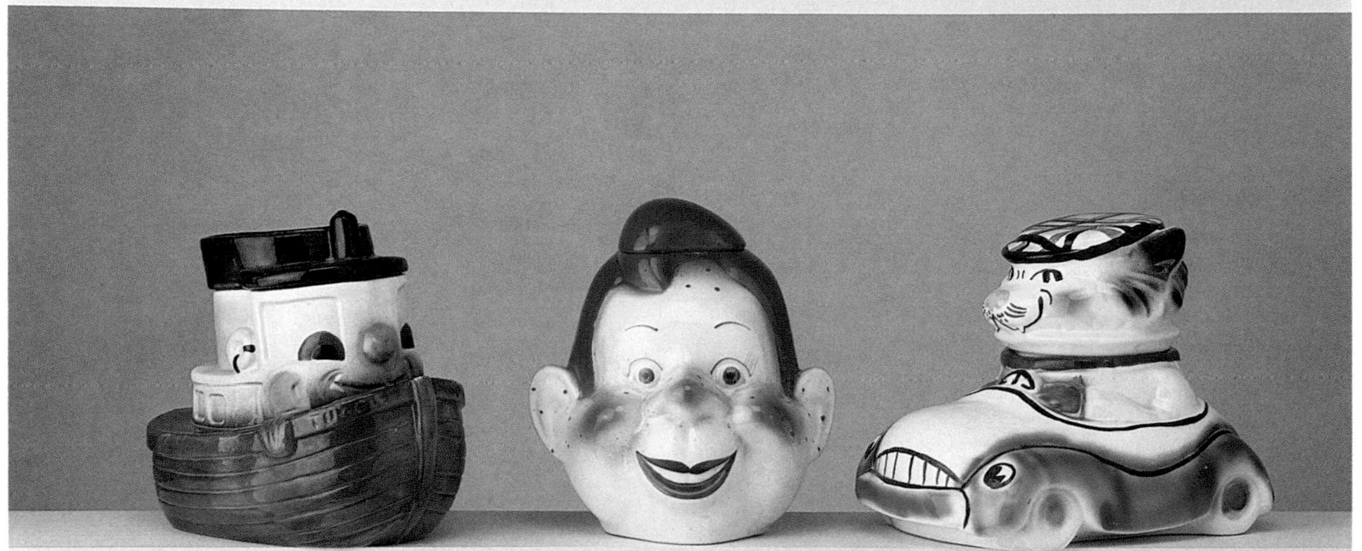

ROW 1:	*Marsh Pig with Apple,* unmarked (1967). Marsh Ceramics is a division of Marsh Industries located in Los Angeles, California	$25.00-30.00
	Hippo, unmarked	$28.00-32.00
	Wind-Up Car, probably California Originals	$28.00-32.00
ROW 2:	*California Originals Cookie Crocodile,* "copyright 862"	$28.00-32.00
	California Originals Raggedy Ann, "859"	$35.00-40.00
	Space Cadet, unmarked	$35.00-40.00
ROW 3:	*Indian,* "Maurice of California"	$28.00-32.00
	Rabbit, "copyright Elmer"	$25.00-30.00
	Red Bull or *Ferdinand?* unmarked, possibly Disney	$50.00-60.00

SPACE CADET

ROW 1:	*Cookie Sack,* "201," ABC	$20.00-25.00
	Train Engine, "200," ABC	$25.00-30.00
	Cookie Clock, "203," ABC	$20.00-25.00
ROW 2:	*Franciscan Nun,* unmarked	$80.00-90.00
	House, unmarked	$20.00-25.00
	Monk, unmarked	$30.00-35.00

The *Deer* and *Poodle* cookie jars pictured on the third row were made by American Bisque. The *Clown* has been "dubbed" *Pinky Lee* and is also available with a pink hat. If this jar is Pinky Lee, where are the checks, and isn't the bow tie just a little conservative for him?

ROW 3:	*Deer,* unmarked	$25.00-30.00
	Poodle, unmarked	$25.00-30.00
	Clown Head, unmarked	$28.00-32.00

All of the above cookie jars sit on horseshoe-shaped bases, which is not common to ABC. However, the horseshoe on the *Clown* is wider and reversed.

COOKIE RR.
COOKIE TIME
Thou shalt not steal!

ROW 1:	*Monk,* "Japan"	$20.00-25.00
	Milk Can, unmarked	$25.00-28.00
	Stove, unmarked	$15.00-18.00
ROW 2:	*Candy Baby,* ABC, has the same horseshoe-shaped base as *Deer* and *Dog* shown previously	$30.00-35.00
	Rag Doll, unmarked	$35.00-40.00
	Clown, "Wedges," not ABC	$55.00-65.00
ROW 3:	*Pretzel finial cookie jar,* "USA"	$18.00-22.00
	Cookie Canister, "Marcrest, oven proof, USA," actually a Hull product manufactured for Marshall Burns	$18.00-22.00
	Cookie Bucket, wooden, unmarked	$12.00-15.00

COOKIES
5 GAL
PURE
MILK
Cookies
Help
Yourself

ROW 1:	Marsh *Bear on Blocks,* Catalog #493, 1967	$38.00-42.00
	Ludowici Celadon *Fluffy Cat,* "Fluffy" in script	$35.00-40.00
	R2-D2, "copyright 1977, 20th Century-Fox Film Corp." Made by Roman Ceramics, Mayfield, Kentucky.	$110.00-120.00
ROW 2:	*Baby Chick,* unmarked	$28.00-32.00
	Matching *Baby Chick* salt and pepper, unmarked	$8.00-10.00
	White Hen, unmarked	$15.00-18.00
	Baby Duck, unmarked	$28.00-32.00
	Matching *Baby Duck* salt and pepper, unmarked	$8.00-10.00
ROW 3:	*Clown,* unmarked	$18.00-22.00
	Clown, "YONG Original, copyright USA Northfork College"	$28.00-32.00
	Penguin, unmarked	$18.00-22.00
	Humpty Dumpty, unmarked	$28.00-32.00

A B C
COOKIES

ROW 1:	*Clown Head,* "Italy," possibly wrong lid	$28.00-32.00
	Lion, "Made in Italy, 4960"	$28.00-32.00
ROW 2:	*B. C.*, unmarked glass jar	$28.00-32.00
	Roly Poly Santa, unmarked	$30.00-35.00
	Churn, "Lane USA"	$18.00-22.00
ROW 3:	*Cat with Hands in Pocket,* "USA" back of base	$35.00-40.00
	Lamb, unmarked	$28.00-32.00
	Cat with Hands in Pockets, "USA" back of base	$35.00-40.00

Both cats with hands in pockets are American Bisque.

FOR GOOD LITTLE
LAMBS ONLY

ROW 1:	*Cat with Ball of Yarn,* "CJ 1 USA"	$25.00-30.00
	Gingerbread Boys, unmarked	$15.00-18.00
	Train, unmarked	$18.00-22.00
ROW 2:	*Clown,* "USA, CJ 4"	$18.00-22.00
	Sheriff on Safe, "CJ USA"	$25.00-28.00
	Milk Can, "KJ 10"	$15.00-18.00
ROW 3:	*Sheriff,* "USA," probably California Originals	$28.00-32.00
	Sheriff, unmarked	$28.00-32.00
	Pirate, unmarked, possibly an ice bucket	$28.00-32.00

Kookie Kat
Kookie Klown
COOKIE SAFE
COOKIES and MILK are YUMMY
SHERIFF

ROW 1: *Hopalong Cassidy,* unmarked, decal of Hopalong Cassidy is missing from the front of this jar, has been found with "Peter Pan Products, Inc., Chicago, Illinois" paper label. $175.00-185.00

Hopalong Cassidy, unmarked $300.00-350.00

Howdy Doody Cookie Tin. The knob is filled with a desiccant to ensure freshness. $50.00-60.00

ROW 2: *Cookie Monster* glass container, "copyright Muppets" $20.00-25.00

Betty Boop, "copyright 1983 KFS, Inc.," paper label: "Vandor, Made in Japan" $40.00-50.00

Mopsey, "copyright Mopsey" $28.00-32.00

ROW 3: *Big Bird on Nest,* "Demand Marketing, Henderson, Ky., Made in USA, copyright, MUPPETS, INC." $28.00-32.00

Oscar the Grouch, unmarked, but also made by Demand Marketing $28.00-32.00

Cookie Chef, "Demand Marketing, Henderson, KY. Made in U.S.A., copyright, MUPPETS, INC." $28.00-32.00

BELOW: *Elf House with Tumbling Elf Figures,* unknown $38.00-42.00

Car with Flat Tire, Fitz & Floyd $50.00-60.00

HOWDY DOODY
cookie-go-round

COOKIES
COOKIE
CHEF

ROW 1: *Churn Boy,* unmarked, made by Regal China $70.00-80.00

German Gentleman, "Made in Western Germany 3802" $40.00-50.00

C-3PO, "Star Wars TM, copyright 1977, U.S.A., Twentieth Century-Fox Film Corporation," made by Roman Ceramics $90.00-100.00

ROW 2: *Astronaut,* "USA," made by McCoy in 1963 $85.00-90.00

Baking Angel, unmarked $75.00-80.00

Grandma, "California USA" $65.00-70.00

ROW 3: *Tattletale,* "copyright Helen's Tat-L-Tale, Helen Hutula Original S 28" $115.00-125.00

Bugs Bunny, "copyright, Warner Bros. Inc. 1981" $80.00-90.00

Woody Woodpecker, "A3391/ww," Napco $115.00-125.00

BELOW: *Popeye,* paper label: "copyright 1980 KING FEATURES SYNDICATE, INC.," Vandor $100.00-125.00

Sheriff, "Fitz and Floyd" $65.00-75.00

HOME OF
B-BUNNY
"WOODY WOOD PECKER"

ROW 1: *Red Riding Hood,* unmarked $30.00-35.00

Red Riding Hood, unmarked $30.00-35.00

The above two jars are apparently reproductions made from the original Hull mold.

ROW 2: *Snowman,* "copyright, B.C., made in USA" $50.00-55.00

Mrs. Claus, unmarked, but probably an import $30.00-35.00

German Origin Jar, "Made in Germany" $50.00-60.00

ROW 3: *Monk with Key,* unmarked $40.00-45.00

Dutch Girl, unmarked, presumably handmade $20.00-25.00

Kitchen Witch, unmarked $25.00-28.00

ROW 1:	*Porky Pig*, unmarked	$30.00-35.00
	Barefoot Boy, "Arnel's." "Arnel's" is a ceramic mold company.	$40.00-45.00
	Harpo Marx???, unmarked. This jar, dubbed "Harpo Marx," is not a Regal item, according to Donna Zerull, a longtime Regal employee. She further states, "We never made this cookie jar, and have no idea who made it."	$50.00-60.00
ROW 2:	*Elephant*, "copyright Bingo"	$30.00-35.00
	Bubblegum Machine, "890 USA," California Originals	$30.00-35.00
	Cookie Can, unmarked	$15.00-20.00
ROW 3:	*Squirrel*, "Arnel's"	$15.00-20.00
	Clown, unmarked	$25.00-28.00
	Pink Lady, unmarked except for a blue crest stamped on bottom	$20.00-25.00
BELOW:	*Tiger*, unmarked	$40.00-50.00
	Cat and Yarn, unmarked	$40.00-45.00
	Kliban Cat, "taste setter Sigma"	$50.00-55.00

1¢
EACH
COOKIE
CAN
BEWARE
of
BEAR

ROW 1: *Pirate,* unmarked except for "star" on bottom. This is one of a series of jars commonly called "star" jars because of the star-shaped design on the bottom. This series has recently been identified by the Allen family as early American Bisque. $30.00-35.00

Fish, unmarked $30.00-35.00

Chef, unmarked, "star" on bottom, ABC as above $30.00-35.00

ROW 2: *Little Hen,* unmarked $28.00-32.00

Rooster, unmarked $25.00-30.00

Chick with Tulip Hat, unmarked $28.00-32.00

ROW 3: *Coffee Grinder,* unmarked $20.00-25.00

Elf Head, unmarked $38.00-42.00

Piano, unmarked $20.00-25.00

BELOW: *Children on Windmill,* "Tulip Tyme 19261" $50.00-60.00

Jonah on Whale, unmarked $70.00-80.00

Children on Drum, "1957 Yona Original" $50.00-60.00

ROW 1:	*Avon House,* probably part of a canister set	$38.00-42.00
	Avon Cookie Jar with Avon lady at the door	$60.00-70.00
	Hand Painted Pink Depression Glass, unmarked	$30.00-35.00
ROW 2:	*Hall China Cookie Jar*	$38.00-42.00
	Hall Autumn Leaf, "Hall's Superior Quality Kitchenware Tested and approved by Mary Dunbar Jewel Homemakers' Institute"	$120.00-130.00
	Hand Painted Green Depression Glass, unmarked	$30.00-35.00
ROW 3:	*Strawberry Shortcake,* "MCML XXXIII, American Greetings Corp., Cleveland, Ohio"	$40.00-50.00
	Strawberry Shortcake mug	$12.00-15.00
	Garfield, "Garfield, copyright, 1982 United Feature Syndicate Inc. Licensed Enesco." There is also a small gold Enesco label on the bottom.	$48.00-52.00
	Cathy, "copyright 1982 Universal Press Syndicate, copyright George-GOOD Corporation," also has a gold paper label stating "Made in Taiwan"	$48.00-52.00
BELOW:	*Halo Boy,* "De Forrest of Calif. copyright 1956"	$70.00-80.00
	Chef, "Hand Painted Pottery Guild of America"	$65.00-75.00

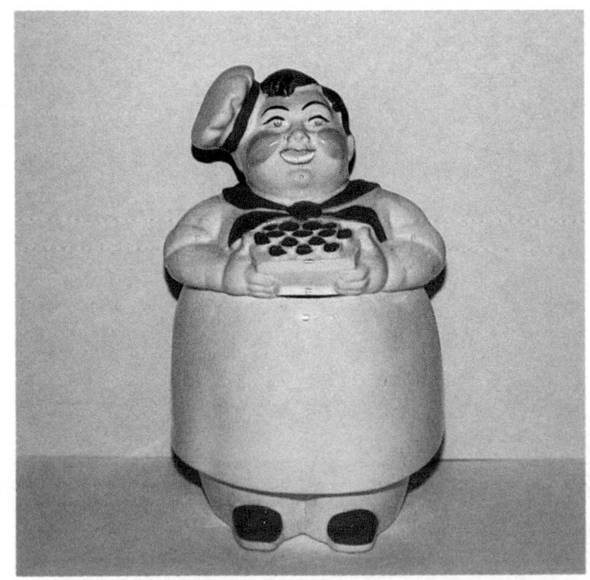

KEEP YOUR HANDS
OFF MY COOKIES!

ROW 1:	*Bear on Beehive,* unmarked	$18.00-22.00
	Cookie Bear, unmarked	$20.00-25.00
	Bear with Cookie Hive, unmarked	$18.00-22.00
ROW 2:	*Colonial Man,* unmarked	$60.00-65.00
	Colonial Woman, unmarked	$60.00-65.00
	Churn Boy, unmarked, lighter weight than ABC and Regal China	$38.00-42.00
ROW 3:	*Oriental Man,* unmarked	$42.00-48.00
	Hooky Cookie, "Rag-R Krn," brass ring in lid	$75.00-85.00
	Koo Kee, "Maker of Cookies," Chinese writing inside lid	$35.00-45.00
BELOW:	*Heart,* "The California Cleminsons, copyright"	$50.00-60.00
	Campbell Kid Nodder, unmarked	$60.00-70.00
	Mother Goose, "Gilner USA G-720"	$65.00-75.00

COOKIES
BEAR
COOKIE HIVE
NO HOOKY COOKY

ROW 1:	*Wilbur, the Blue Ribbon Pig,* unmarked	$35.00-40.00
	Red Pig, unmarked	$28.00-32.00
	Rooster, unmarked	$20.00-25.00
ROW 2:	*Clover Rabbit,* unmarked	$25.00-28.00
	Plastic Pig, unmarked Aladdin product	$15.00-20.00
	Rocking Horse, unmarked	$15.00-18.00
ROW 3:	*Cookie Girl,* "USA 202," American Bisque	$20.00-25.00
	Chef, unmarked	$15.00-18.00
	Chef salt and pepper, unmarked	$5.00-8.00
	Smile Face, unmarked, and probably the wrong lid	$20.00-25.00

"COOKIE"

Pottery Guild

Pottery Guild of America was manufactured by the Cronin China Company in Minerva, Ohio, during the late 1930's and the early 1940's. These semi-porcelain cookie jars were manufactured for the Block China Company, which was, and is, a selling agency.

Probably the most popular and sought after Pottery Guild piece is *Elsie, the Borden Cow,* manufactured for the Borden Company in the late 1940's. (See Advertisement Section.)

ROW 1:	*Dutch Girl,* "Hand Painted Pottery Guild, Made in America"	$40.00-45.00
	Red Riding Hood, unmarked	$80.00-85.00
	Dutch Boy, unmarked	$40.00-45.00
ROW 2:	*Dutch Girl,* unmarked	$40.00-45.00
	Little Girl, unmarked	$45.00-50.00
	Dutch Boy, unmarked	$40.00-45.00
ROW 3:	*Rooster,* "Hand Painted Pottery Guild of America"	$38.00-42.00
	Balloon Lady, unmarked	$68.00-72.00
	Apple, unmarked	$18.00-22.00

The *Apple* may not be Pottery Guild. We originally thought it was because of the way the lid is designed; now, we are doubtful.

Red Wing

The roots of the Red Wing Pottery go very deeply into the 1800's, but it was not until the 1920's that Red Wing produced its first cookie jars.

One of Red Wing's earliest cookie jars is illustrated in the white crock shown on row one. Dolores Simon's *Red Wing Pottery with Rumrill* shows #21 as part of its identifying mark.

The *Bob White* cookie jar, with matching salt and pepper shakers, was part of a very popular dinnerware set produced in 1966.

Red Wing was forced to permanently close its doors in 1967 after a lengthy labor dispute.

ROW 1:	*Peasant Design,* unmarked. This cookie jar and the munch jar in the bottom row were featured in the July, 1943 *Better Homes and Gardens.*	$28.00-32.00
	Dutch Girl, stamped "Red Wing," also "Red Wing USA" impressed into the bottom of the jar	$55.00-60.00
	White Crock, bottom discolored, mark not legible, listed as #21 as discussed above	$20.00-25.00
ROW 2:	*Grapes,* "Red Wing USA"	$38.00-42.00
	Bob White, unmarked	$60.00-65.00
	Bob White salt and pepper shakers, unmarked	$12.00-15.00
	Pineapple, "Red Wing"	$35.00-40.00
ROW 3:	*Carrousel,* unmarked	$115.00-125.00
	Jack Frost, unmarked	$125.00-150.00
	Peasant Design Munch Jar, unmarked	$25.00-30.00

In later years, Red Wing marked part of its cookie jars with labels and few have survived to aid in identification. We have seen the taller version of *Jack Frost* with the label.

ROW 1:	*Chef,* "Red Wing USA"	$65.00-75.00
	Chef, unmarked	$50.00-60.00
	Chef, unmarked	$50.00-60.00
ROW 2:	*Monk,* unmarked	$50.00-60.00
	Monk, "Red Wing, USA"	$50.00-60.00
	Monk, "Red Wing, USA"	$50.00-60.00
ROW 3:	*King of Tarts,* "Red Wing, USA"	$130.00-140.00
	King of Tarts, "Red Wing USA"	$150.00-160.00
	King of Tarts, unmarked	$110.00-120.00

TARTS

Regal China

Ruth Van Telligen Bendel has made her mark in history, not only among cookie jar collectors for her irresistible *Peek-a-Boo* cookie jar, but also among salt and pepper collectors for her *Snuggle-Hugs* salt and pepper shaker sets.

Bendel is an art illustrator who draws illustrations for children's magazines, decal designs for baby furniture, etc. Her love for children further shines through in her patented designs for Regal.

The *Peek-a-Boo* was the only cookie jar she designed. Approximately 1,400 to 1,800 of these were produced by the Regal/Royal China and Novelty Company.

The *Snuggle-Hugs* were salt and peppers produced under both the Van Telligen and Bendel names. The original patent application was dated May 6, 1949. The Van Telligen items are all marked "Patent Pending," while the items marked "Bendel" all carry the patent number "2560755" and are dated "1958."

ROW 1:	*Snuggle-Hug Boy and Dog,* Van Telligen	$35.00-38.00
	Snuggle-Hug Boy and Dog, Van Telligen	$35.00-38.00
	Single Rabbit, "copr. 1958 R. BENDEL"	$10.00-12.00
	Double or Nothing Pig Shakers, also available as banks, "copr. 1958, R. BENDEL, PAT. NO. 2560755"	$75.00-85.00
	Love Bugs, small, BENDEL	$35.00-38.00
	Love Bugs, large, "copyright BENDEL - LOVE BUG, PAT. NO. 54-185B"	$45.00-48.00
ROW 2:	*Snuggle-Hug Dutch Boy and Girl,* Van Telligen	$25.00-28.00
	Peek-a-Boo small shakers, "copyright Van Telligen"	$35.00-45.00
	Peek-a-Boo cookie jar, "Peek-a-Boo, copyright Van Telligen"	$325.00-350.00
	Peek-a-Boo shakers, large, "Van Telligen copyright, PAT. PEND. PEEK-A-BOO"	$60.00-70.00
	Snuggle-Hug Sailor and Mermaid, Van Telligen	$55.00-60.00
ROW 3:	*Snuggle-Hug Ducks,* Van Telligen	$25.00-28.00
	Snuggle-Hug Rabbits, unknown, not Van Telligen	$18.00-22.00
	Snuggle-Hug Rabbits, Van Telligen	$18.00-22.00
	Snuggle-Hug Rabbits, Van Telligen	$18.00-22.00
	Snuggle-Hug Rabbits, Van Telligen	$18.00-22.00
ROW 4:	*Snuggle-Hug Bears,* Van Telligen	$18.00-22.00
	Snuggle-Hug Bears, Van Telligen	$18.00-22.00
	Snuggle-Hug Bears, Van Telligen	$18.00-22.00
	Snuggle-Hug Girl and Lamb	$25.00-28.00
	Snuggle-Hug Girl and Lamb	$25.00-28.00
	Snuggle-Hug Girl and Lamb	$25.00-28.00

ROW 1: *Dutch Girl,* "54-200." Matching salt and pepper shakers are also available. $140.00-150.00

Alice salt shaker, "Alice in Wonderland" $70.00-75.00

Alice in Wonderland, "Walt Disney Productions, copyright, Alice in Wonderland," produced in the 1950's $500.00 & up

White Rabbit creamer, "Walt Disney Productions, copyright, White Rabbit" $50.00-60.00

Fi Fi, "copyright C. Miller 1163" $180.00-200.00

ROW 2: *Whaler* or *Fisherman,* unmarked $225.00-250.00

Rocking Horse, "Hobby Horse #706" $85.00-95.00

Miss Muffet, "Little Miss Muffet, #705" $85.00-95.00

ROW 3: *French Chef,* "54-192." Matching salt and pepper shakers are also available. $85.00-95.00

Oriental Lady with baskets, unmarked $170.00-180.00

Wolf Jar, unmarked $385.00-395.00

Toby Cookies, unmarked $185.00-195.00

TOBY COOKIES

"Old MacDonald Had A Farm, E-i-ee-i-Oh"

ROW1:	*Feed Sacks with Sheep* salt and pepper, "Pat. Pending 384"	$30.00-40.00
	Tid Bit canister, large, "Pat. Pending 387," lid "394"	$90.00-100.00
	Peanuts canister, large, "Pat. Pending 387" base, lid mark is not legible	$90.00-100.00
	Cookie canister, large, "Pat. Pending 387" base, lid "394"	$90.00-100.00
	Pig grease jar, "Pat. Pending 386"	$40.00-50.00
ROW 2:	*Sugar* canister, small, "Pat. Pending 389" base, lid "413"	$75.00-85.00
	Tea canister, small, "Pat. Pending 389" base, lid "414"	$75.00-85.00
	Cereal canister, small, "Pat. Pending 389" base, lid "417"	$75.00-85.00
	Salt canister, "Pat. Pending 389" base, lid not legible	$75.00-85.00
	Coffee canister, "Pat. Pending 389" base, lid "414"	$75.00-85.00

Mrs. MacDonald and the *Horse* lids are also available for the small canisters. A *Flour* canister is also available in the small size.

ROW 3:	*Churn* salt and pepper, "Pat. Pending 385"	$20.00-25.00
	Pepper jar, "Pat. Pending 390," lid "410"	$35.00-40.00
	Cloves jar, "Pat. Pending 390," lid "408"	$35.00-40.00
	Spice jar, "Pat. Pending 390," lid "407"	$35.00-40.00
	Nutmeg jar, "Pat. Pending 390," lid not legible	$35.00-40.00
	Allspice jar, "Pat. Pending 390," lid "411"	$35.00-40.00
	Cinnamon jar, "Pat. Pending 390," lid "409"	$35.00-40.00
	Boy and Girl salt and pepper, "Pat. Pending 392"	$28.00-32.00
ROW 4:	*Hen on Nest* sugar bowl, "Pat. Pending 382"	$38.00-42.00
	Rooster creamer, "Pat. Pending 383"	$38.00-42.00
	Cow butter dish, "Pat. Pending 388"	$50.00-60.00
	Duck teapot, "Pat. Pending 391"	$125.00-135.00
	Barn cookie jar, "Pat. Pending 381"	$100.00-110.00
BELOW:	*Flour* canister, "Pat. Pending 389" base, lid "416"	$75.00-85.00
	Milk pitcher, "Pat. Pending 380"	$190.00-200.00
	Popcorn canister, "Pat. Pending 387," lid not legible	$90.00-100.00

SALT
COFFEE

ROW 1:	*Lion Bank,* paper label: "made by The Lefton China Co., Japan"	$18.00-22.00
	Hubert the Lion, produced for the Harris Bank in Chicago, Illinois, in December, 1982. "Hubert, Made in USA." Hubert was produced in limited numbers of approximately 1,500.	$225.00-250.00
	Majorette, unmarked	$125.00-135.00
ROW 2:	*Quaker Oats,* marked "Regal" under the recipe	$110.00-115.00
	Goldilocks, "405 Goldilocks, Pat. Pending"	$120.00-130.00
	Goldilocks salt and pepper shakers, unmarked	$50.00-55.00
	Diaper Pin Pig, "404"	$150.00-175.00
ROW 3:	*Davy Crockett,* "Translucent Vitrified China, copyright, C. Miller 55-140 B"	$140.00-150.00
	Cat, unmarked	$125.00-135.00
	Cat salt and pepper shakers.There is also a matching sugar and creamer set.	$35.00-40.00
	Clown, "Translucent Vitrified China, copyright, C. Miller 54-439 A"	$115.00-125.00

OLD FASHIONED
QUAKER
OATS
DAVY
CROCKETT

Robinson-Ransbottom

The Robinson-Ransbottom Pottery Company of Roseville, Ohio, has been in operation since 1901.

For many years, starting in about 1935, Robinson-Ransbottom produced cookie jars hand-decorated in cold paint and glazed in freehand decorations. W.L. Pace was the chief decorator from 1935 until 1955 with the distinction of being the first decorator of cookie jars in the area.

An interesting note from Donald D. Pace, Vice President of Sales for the Robinson-Ransbottom Pottery Company in 1974 revealed, "The first cookie jars around here were made by decorating preserve jars - the same shape which Grandma used for preserving vegetables, fruit, and meats. (The preserve jar cover was sealed with sealing wax.)"

Robinson-Ransbottom is still in business but no longer produces cookie jars. In the aforementioned letter, Pace stated, "Our company quit making cookie jars due to the increasing demand for products we were making more or less exclusively."

ROW 1:	*Chef,* gold-trimmed, "RRP Co. Roseville, Ohio 411"	$75.00-85.00
	Sheriff Pig, gold-trimmed, "RRP Co. Roseville, Ohio 363"	$75.00-85.00
	Ol' King Cole, "RRP Co. Roseville, Ohio"	$65.00-75.00
ROW 2:	*Dutch Boy,* unmarked	$55.00-65.00
	Whale, "RRP Co. Roseville, Ohio"	$115.00-125.00
	Dutch Girl, "RRP Co. Roseville, Ohio"	$55.00-65.00
ROW 3:	*Peter, Peter, Pumpkin Eater,* "RRP Co. Roseville, Ohio 1502"	$60.00-65.00
	Hi Diddle Diddle, gold-trimmed, "RRP Co. Roseville, Ohio 317"	$70.00-80.00
	Tigers, "RRP Co. Roseville, Ohio 386"	$35.00-45.00

ROW 1: *Brownie,* "USA" and "Brownie" on collar. This jar was not produced by Robinson-Ransbottom as we earlier believed. It is an American Bisque production, confirmed by A.N. Allen. $35.00-40.00

Some personal correspondence from Edna Myers states, contrary to popular belief, RRP made only *Oscar the Doughboy* in what is believed to be a series. The statement was confirmed by J.C. Woodward, president of Robinson-Ransbottom Pottery in 1982.

Oscar, unmarked except for name, shown in 1943 *Crown Pottery* (Robinson-Ransbottom) catalog $35.00-40.00

Cop, "USA," made by American Bisque $35.00-40.00

ROW 2: *Jack,* unmarked, shown in 1943 catalog $50.00-60.00

Bud, unmarked, shown in 1943 catalog $50.00-60.00

Frosty the Snowman, "RRP Co. Roseville O, USA" $100.00-110.00

ROW 3: *Sheriff Pig,* "RRP Co. Roseville, Ohio 363" $35.00-40.00

Hootie Owl, "RRP Co. Roseville, O 359" $35.00-40.00

Jocko the Monkey "RRP Co. Roseville, O USA" $60.00-65.00

Shawnee

The Shawnee Pottery Company, named for an American Indian tribe, was located in Zanesville, Ohio. It began operation in 1937 and continued until 1961.

Interestingly, Addis E. Hull, whose father founded the Hull Company, left Hull to manage the new company.

George Rumrill was a jobber and designer from Little Rock, Arkansas, who designed RUM RILL and engaged Shawnee to produce it for him. George was one of Shawnee's more prominent customers and it was due to this connection that Rudy Gantz, the designer of *Smiley Pig*, was employed by Shawnee.

Great Northern, Kenwood, and Essex China are other product names of Shawnee.

ROW 1: *Great Northern Dutch Boy,* "Great Northern USA 1025" $120.00-130.00

Winnie Bank/Cookie Jar, "Patented Winnie Shawnee USA 61" $140.00-150.00

Smiley Bank/Cookie Jar, "Patented Smiley 60 Shawnee USA" $120.00-130.00

ROW 2: *Great Northern Dutch Girl,* "Great Northern USA 1026" $100.00-110.00

Winnie Bank/Cookie Jar, "Patented Winnie Shawnee USA 61" $140.00-150.00

Smiley Bank/Cookie Jar, "Patented Smiley 60 Shawnee USA" $120.00-130.00

ROW 3: *Tulip Smiley* with gold trim, "USA" $140.00-150.00

Clover Bloom Winnie, "Winnie USA" $110.00-120.00

Clover Smiley, "Patented Smiley USA" $75.00-85.00

Winnie and Smiley salt and pepper set, gold-trimmed, 3 inch $22.00-25.00

ROW 1: *Cottage,* "USA 6." There are range-size salt and pepper shakers to go with the *Cottage.* Joyce has seen them with *Essex China* paper labels. $100.00-125.00

Elephant, "USA" $28.00-32.00

Little Chef, gold-trimmed, "USA" $75.00-85.00

ROW 2: *Dutch Boy,* "USA" $30.00-38.00

Dutch Girl, "USA" $35.00-40.00

Dutch Boy, "USA" $30.00-38.00

ROW 3: *Dutch Girl,* "USA" $35.00-40.00

Dutch Boy, "USA" $30.00-38.00

Dutch Girl, "USA" $35.00-40.00

All of the above cookie jars, with the exception of the *Cottage* and the *Little Chef,* are the early Shawnee jars decorated with cold paint.

COOKIES

ROW 1:	*Mugsey,* gold and decals, "Patented Mugsey USA"	$175.00-185.00
	Mugsey, gold trim, salt and pepper shakers, range size	$42.00-45.00
	Mugsey, "USA"	$90.00-100.00
	Mugsey, salt and pepper, undecorated, range-size	$38.00-42.00
	Mugsey, salt and pepper, undecorated, small	$20.00-22.00
	Mugsey, gold and decals, "Patented Mugsey USA"	$175.00-185.00
	Mugsey, salt and pepper, decorated, small	$30.00-35.00
ROW 2:	*Puss 'n Boots,* gold and decals, "Patented Puss 'n Boots USA"	$160.00-170.00
	Puss 'n Boots, salt and pepper, gold and decals, small	$20.00-25.00
	Puss 'n Boots, gold and decals, "Patented Puss 'n Boots USA"	$160.00-170.00
	Puss 'n Boots, salt and pepper, undecorated	$18.00-20.00
	Puss 'n Boots, gold and decals, "Patented Puss 'n Boots USA"	$160.00-170.00
	Puss 'n Boots, salt and pepper, gold and decals, small	$20.00-25.00
ROW 3:	*Owl,* "USA"	$70.00-80.00
	Owl, salt and pepper, small, unmarked	$12.00-15.00
	Lucky Elephant, gold and decals, "USA"	$165.00-175.00
	Owl, gold and hand-decorated, "USA"	$160.00-170.00
	Owl, salt and pepper, gold and hand-decorated, unmarked	$20.00-25.00

Most of the Shawnee salt and pepper sets are unmarked.

We have been told many times over the years that the decorated Shawnee cookie jars were seconds that had been salvaged. This is definitely a possibility after closely examining our jars. *Lucky Elephant* has a fly on his trunk to hide a flaw and the glaze appears to be just a little rough.

Whatever the incentive behind the designs, we are glad the decision was made. How could a collection be complete without these beautiful jars?

ROW 1:	*Smiley,* gold and decals, "USA"	$140.00-150.00
	Winnie, gold-trimmed, "USA." We remember when we first received this *Winnie.* Joyce tried in vain to clean off the red paint she was sure someone had applied, possibly to match their decor. No luck; it wouldn't budge; it belonged.	$155.00-165.00
	Winnie and Smiley, salt and pepper, range-size	$32.00-38.00
	Smiley, gold-trimmed, "USA"	$140.00-150.00
ROW 2:	*Smiley,* gold and decals, "USA"	$140.00-150.00
	Smiley, salt and pepper, unmarked	$18.00-22.00
	Winnie, gold-trimmed, "Patented Winnie USA"	$140.00-150.00
	Smiley, gold and decals, "USA"	$140.00-150.00
	Smiley, salt and pepper with gold and decals, range size	$38.00-42.00
ROW 3:	*Smiley,* "USA"	$75.00-85.00
	Winnie, "USA"	$110.00-120.00
	Smiley, salt and pepper, range-size	$32.00-38.00
	Smiley, "USA." Notice the black hooves and buttons.	$75.00-85.00

ROW 1:	*Cookie,* gold and decals, "USA"	$140.00-150.00
	Happy, gold and decals, "USA"	$115.00-125.00
	Dutch Boy and *Dutch Girl* salt and pepper, undecorated	$28.00-32.00
	Cookie, gold and decals, "USA"	$140.00-150.00
ROW 2:	*Happy,* gold and decals, "USA"	$115.00-125.00
	Cookie, gold and decals, "USA"	$145.00-155.00
	Happy, gold and decals, "USA"	$115.00-125.00
ROW 3:	*Sailor, "GOB,"* "USA"	$225.00-250.00
	Cookie, gold and decals, "USA"	$145.00-155.00
	Happy, gold and decals, "USA"	$125.00-135.00

USN

ROW 1:	*Little Chef,* "USA"	$30.00-35.00
	Jug, "USA"	$45.00-50.00
	Little Chef, "USA"	$35.00-38.00
ROW 2:	*Octagon with Wheat,* "USA"	$20.00-25.00
	Fruit Basket, "Shawnee 84"	$35.00-45.00
	Corn, "Shawnee 66"	$65.00-70.00
ROW 3:	*Elephant,* "Shawnee 60," available with both black and white cold paint on the collar	$45.00-50.00
	Sailor, "USA"	$35.00-40.00
	Lucky Elephant, "USA"	$25.00-30.00

Salt and pepper shakers are available in two sizes to match the *Corn* cookie jar. There are also matching shakers to the *Fruit Basket.* The *Shawnee Sailor* shaker is not an exact replica of the cookie jar.

COOKIES
COOKIES

Sierra Vista

Sierra Vista began as a family venture with co-ownership by Reinhold Lenaburg and his son Leonard. The business originated in Sierra Vista, California, in 1942 and continued until 1951, when Reinhold retired and sold his part of the business to Leonard. After assuming ownership, Leonard moved the business to Phoenix, Arizona, and continued to use the founding name.

ROW 1:	*Train,* "Sierra Vista, California"	$35.00-40.00
	Circus Wagon, "Sierra Vista Ceramics, Pasadena, California USA copyright 1957"	$55.00-60.00
	Elephant, "Sierra Vista of California"	$30.00-35.00
ROW 2:	*Davy Crocket,* "Sierra Vista of Calif., copyright"	$140.00-150.00
	Poodle, "Sierra Vista Ceramics, Pasadena, Calif. copyright 1956"	$55.00-60.00
	Stage Coach, "Sierra Vista Ceramics, Pasadena, Calif., USA, copyright 1956"	$75.00-80.00
ROW 3:	*Rooster,* "Sierra Vista, California"	$30.00-35.00
	Squirrel, "Sierra Vista, California"	$35.00-40.00
	Clown, "Sierra Vista, California"	$28.00-32.00

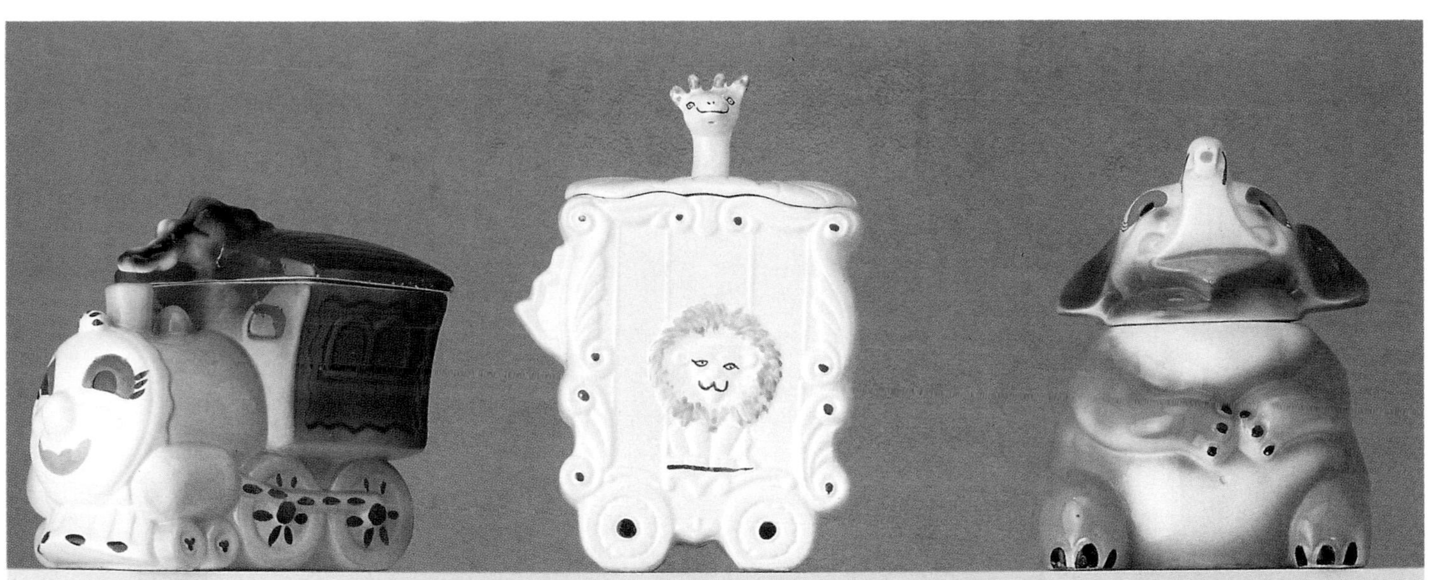

Treasure Craft

The Treasure Craft Company of Compton, California, was founded by Alfred A. Levin in 1945. The Levin family owned and operated the business until November 1988, when the company was purchased by Pfaltzfgraff of York, Pennsylvania.

The company is currently producing high quality, well-designed cookie jars. The cookie jars being produced for the Hallmark "Auntie Em" series is but one example. These are the collectibles of tomorrow.

ROW 1: *Rocking Horse,* "Treasure Craft, copyright Made in USA" $25.00-28.00

Owl, "Treasure Craft, Made in USA" $18.00-22.00

Sailor Elephant, unmarked $20.00-25.00

ROW 2: *Hobo,* label, "Treasure Craft Compton, California Made in USA" $28.00-32.00

Mouse, "Treasure Craft, copyright USA" $25.00-30.00

Chef, "Treasure Craft, copyright USA" $20.00-25.00

ROW 3: *Puppy,* "Treasure Craft, copyright USA" $25.00-30.00

Farmer Pig, "Treasure Craft, copyright USA." The *Farmer Pig* is still carried in the 1989 catalog. $28.00-32.00

Teddy Bear, "Treasure Craft, copyright USA." The *Teddy Bear* is also shown in the 1989 catalog. $28.00-32.00

COOKIES
U.S.N.

COOKIE CHEF

ROW 1:	*Dog,* "Treasure Craft Compton, Calif., Made in USA"	$18.00-22.00
	Cat, "Treasure Craft 1968 copyright Compton, Calif."	$20.00-25.00
	Monkey, "Treasure Craft 1968 copyright Compton, Calif."	$18.00-22.00
ROW 2:	*Monk,* "Treasure Craft copyright, Made in USA"	$28.00-32.00
	Bear, "Treasure Craft USA"	$18.00-22.00
	Duck, label only: "Pottery Craft Compton, California 90222. Handcrafted stoneware"	$20.00-25.00
ROW 3:	*Ark,* "Treasure Craft copyright, made in USA" on lid	$28.00-32.00
	Trolley, "Treasure Craft copyright, made in USA"	$28.00-32.00
	Ice Wagon, "Treasure Craft copyright USA"	$35.00-40.00
BELOW:	*Stitch in Time Cat,* unmarked. This jar is from the "Auntie Em Collection," which is a trademark of Hallmark.	$35.00-40.00
	Sugar, unmarked. *Sugar* is the mate to *Spice* shown in the Black Americana section.	$35.00-40.00
	Duck Decoy, unmarked	$35.00-40.00

COOKIES

THOU
SHALT
NOT
STEAL
(COOKIES)

COOKIE
TROLLEY
HOME
ICE
CO.
ESTAB 1902

ROW 1: *Cookieville,* "Treasure Craft, copyright Made in USA" $25.00-30.00

House, "Treasure Craft, copyright Made in USA." The *House* is listed in the 1989 catalog. $25.00-30.00

Cookie Barn, "Treasure Craft, copyright USA."The *Cookie Barn* is also in the 1989 catalog. $25.00-30.00

ROW 2: *Grandfather Clock,* "Treasure Craft, copyright Made in USA" $30.00-35.00

Teddy Bear, "Treasure Craft, copyright USA" in lid, and "Pottery Craft, Compton, Cal. 90222, Handcrafted Stoneware" on base $25.00-30.00

Radio, "Treasure Craft, copyright USA" in lid and on label on base $28.00-32.00

ROW 3: *Butterfly Crock,* "Treasure Craft, copyright Made in USA" in lid and on base $18.00-22.00

Farmer Pig, "Treasure Craft, copyright USA" in lid, and "Pottery Craft, Compton, Ca. 90222" on bottom $28.00-32.00

Coffee Pot, "Treasure Craft, copyright Made in USA," in lid and on base $18.00-22.00

Pottery Craft is the stoneware division of Treasure Craft. The items marked "Treasure Craft" are earthenware. Note the bisque appearance of the *Teddy Bear.*

Pages 276 thru 279 are catalog reprints of Treasure Craft.

COOKIEVILLE
COOKIE BARN
COOKIES
COOKIES

350-80
362-80
353-80
342-80
352-80
368-80
COOKIES
347-80
THOU SHALT NOT STEAL (COOKIES)
343-80
349-80
349-81
351-80
COOKIE CHEF
345-80
COOKIEVILLE
354-80
HANDCRAFTED IN USA
T01-1284

Noël
732-25
414-25
725-25
710-25
164-25
287-25•
288-80
740-25
731-25•
729-25••
728-25•••
40-25
Treasure Craft
998-25
716-25
874-25
717-25
719-25
741-25
742-25
© TIC
Holiday Rose
420-21
525-21
874-21
244-21
521-21
998-21
Treasure Craft
731-21•
540-21
Winter Quilt
420-16
521-16
525-16
731-16
540-16
874-16
998-16
Treasure Craft
246-16
516-16
233-16
971-16
235-16
© B&D
Accessories
286-80
280-80
383-80
419-80
378-80
540-27
609-85
610-85

420-99 (6 Asst.)
424-99
423-99
426-99
CALORIE JAR
I CAN'T BELIEVE I ATE THE WHOLE JAR!
FRESH BAKED
COOKIES
COOKIES
COOKIE TIME
Chew Chew Train
428-99
425-99
422-99
HANDCRAFTED IN USA

346-80
358-80
COOKIES
363-80
370-05
350-80
348-80
341-80
360-12
377-04
367-80
COOKIE TIME
345-80
376-23
374-80
372-80
631-80
365-80

380-07
373-80
352-80
379-80
382-80
349-80
COOKIE BARN
357-80
THOU SHALT NOT STEAL COOKIES
347-80
362-80
375-80
JACKPOT
355-80
384-80
COOKIES
368-80
392-80
386-80
Treasure Craft
made in U.S.A.
330-80
997-80

420-18
420-12
420-05
420-20
BAKED WITH LOVE
420-04
416-85
Grandma's Cookies
415-85
Mom's Cookies
420-07
424-88
432-85
420-15
444-85
439-85
440-88
442-85
430-88
443-85
445-88
441-88
420-48
420-19
431-85
Friends & Cookies make life better
434-85
COOKIE O' MY HEART
435-85
437-85
427-88
MOM'S
Cookies
425-88
COOKIE TIME
421-88
SWEET LOVIN'
426-88
FRESH BAKED
COOKIES
423-88
Sugar & Spice
TREASURE CRAFT
994-85

Twin Winton

The Twin Winton Company was started in 1936 when Don and Ross Winton, twin brothers, were just sixteen years old. The boys were still in high school when they started their small ceramic business.

The business was thriving, when suddenly they were contacted by a lawyer from Walt Disney Products telling them they could no longer sell their wares because the designs were too similar to the Disney ones, although they were Winton originals.

Later, Disney himself, upon learning the age of the boys and being told the business was their sole means of support, called the lawyer and told him to leave them alone.

Production was halted during the war when the boys joined the military until 1946 when Twin Winton was again established in Pasadena producing the "Hillbilly" line. Bruce Winton, another brother, joined them later in 1946 to assist his artistic brothers with the management of the business.

The business was moved to San Juan Capistrano and El Monte, California, in the early 1950's, with the El Monte plant remaining open until 1964.

Cookie jar production was begun on a very limited scale in 1951 using the wood tone finish.

In 1974, the "Collectors' Series" was introduced. There is a total of 18 jars in the collectors' series.

The gold labels found on the Winton jars were applied from 1964 through 1977 only on the high-glaze finishes.

The production phase of Twin Winton came to a close in 1977 with the sale of the business. The molds were purchased by Treasure Craft and were immediately retired, since they had always been strong competitors of Twin Winton.

ROW 1: *Lion,* 1965 catalog, TW 90, "Twin Winton, copyright, Calif., USA" $30.00-35.00

Lion, "Twin Winton, copyright, San Juan Capistrano, Calif. USA" $30.00-35.00

Persian Kitten, 1965 catalog, TW 44, "Twin Winton Calif. USA, copyright'63" $40.00-45.00

ROW 2: *Happy Bull,* 1965 catalog, TW 95, stamped: "Twin Winton, copyright, Calif., USA" $30.00-35.00

Happy Bull salt and pepper, range size, "Twin Winton, Calif., USA" $15.00-18.00

Cookie Barn, 1975 catalog, Code #41 stamped: "Twin Winton, copyright, California, USA" $30.00-35.00

Cow, 1965 catalog, TW 69 $45.00-50.00

ROW 3: *Teddy Bear,* shown in wood finish in 1965 catalog, "Twin Winton, copyright, California, USA" $40.00-45.00

Ranger Bear, 1975 catalog, Code #84 stamped: "Twin Winton, copyright, San Juan Capistrano, Calif., USA" $35.00-40.00

Ranger Bear salt and pepper, small $12.00-15.00

Ranger Bear, Collectors' Series, 1974 stamped: "Twin Winton, copyright, San Juan Capistrano, Calif., USA," artist initials "J.L." $55.00-60.00

COOKIE BARN

Don Winton is a product of southern California and was reared and schooled in Pasadena, where he began his sculpturing career as a teenager. As a diversified sculptor, he has performed many commissions for the entertainment field as well as for corporations, the toy industry, universities and private individuals.

As a former athlete, Winton has done figures of men and women athletes in almost every sport on the national and international scene with notable commission for the Virginia Slims Tennis Tournament, the P.G.A. Tournament, the John Wooden National Basketball Award, the National Gymnastic Championships and other prestigious events in the sports realm.

In the entertainment field, he has sculptured the Grammy Award, the Country and Western Music Award, the medium-size Emmy Award, special commissions for Walt Disney Productions, Disneyland, Hanna-Barbera Productions and Dell Publishing. One of his best known works is the Mickey Mouse telephone created for General Telephone in connection with Walt Disney Studios. Among his works are the Big Brother Award, the Bob's Big Boy, Olympic Development Award and the YMCA Award.

In the portrait sculpture field his works include John F. Kennedy, Richard Nixon, Senator Hubert Humphrey, Golda Meir, Otis Chandler of the *Los Angeles Times,* Bob Hope, Prime Minister David Ben Gurion of Israel, Ze'ev Jabotinsky, Mayor Teddy Kollek of Jerusalem, Alexis de Tocqueville of France and founding Chancellor Daniel Aldrich of the University of California, Irvine.

ROW 1: *Sailor Elephant,* 1965 catalog, TW 86, "Twin Winton, copyright, Made in USA, 60" $30.00-35.00

Sailor Elephant salt and pepper $12.00-15.00

Sailor Elephant wall pocket (Above s&p) "Twin Winton, copyright, Calif., USA" $18.00-22.00

Sailor Elephant bank $18.00-22.00

Sailor Mouse, 1975 catalog, Code #63, "Twin Winton, San Juan Capistrano, Calif., USA." The same code number was assigned to the *Walrus* in the 1965 catalog. $28.00-32.00

ROW 2: *Squirrel,* 1965 catalog, TW 74, "Twin Winton, copyright, El Monte, Calif." $30.00-35.00

Rooster, salt and pepper $15.00-18.00

Rooster, 1975 catalog, "Twin Winton, Collectors' Series, copyright, California, USA" $55.00-60.00

Cookie Nut, 1965 catalog, TW 83, "Twin Winton, copyright, Calif., USA" $28.00-32.00

ROW 3: *Noah's Ark,* shown in 1965 catalog in wood finish, "Twin Winton, Calif., USA" $35.00-38.00

Owl, 1965 catalog, TW 91, "Twin Winton, San Juan Capistrano, Calif. USA," incised and stamped $28.00-32.00

Train, 1965 catalog, TW 89, "Twin Winton, copyright, Calif., USA" $30.00-35.00

COOKIE NUT

97

ROW 1: *Raggedy Andy,* 1975 catalog, Collector' Series, ink stamp, "Twin Winton, San Juan Capistrano, Calif., USA" $55.00-60.00

Raggedy Ann, 1975 catalog, Collectors' Series, ink stamp, "San Juan Capistrano, Calif., USA" $55.00-60.00

Sheriff Bear, 1975 catalog, "Twin Winton Collectors' Series, copyright, California, USA" $55.00-60.00

ROW 2: *Candy Shack,* shown in 1965 catalog $20.00-25.00

Dutch Girl, 1965 catalog, TW 47, "Twin Winton, Calif., USA" $35.00-38.00

Dutch Girl salt and pepper, range-size, unmarked $15.00-18.00

Cookie Elf, 1965 catalog, TW 57, unmarked $30.00-35.00

ROW 3: *Little Lamb,* gold seal: "Beautiful Hand Crafted Ceramics, Made in USA, Twin Winton, California, San Juan Capistrano, Ca. 92675" $30.00-35.00

Squirrel, not shown in either catalog, unmarked $25.00-28.00

Squirrel salt and pepper, small, unmarked $12.00-15.00

Elf Bakery, 1965 catalog, TW 50, Gold seal: "Beautiful Hand Crafted Ceramics, Made in USA, Twin Winton, California San Juan Capistrano, Ca 92675" $25.00-28.00

POLICE

CANDYHOUSE

FOR GOOD LITTLE
LAMBS ONLY
BAKERY

ROW 1: *Donkey,* "Twin Winton, copyright, Calif., USA," featured in 1965 catalog, TW 88 $35.00-40.00

Dobbin, "Twin Winton Made in Calif. USA 1962," featured in 1965 catalog, TW 80 $35.00-40.00

Little Lamb, unmarked, featured in 1965 catalog, TW 66 $30.00-35.00

Little Lamb salt and pepper, range-size $15.00-18.00

ROW 2: *Sheriff Bear,* stamped: "Twin Winton, San Juan Capistrano, Calif. USA," artist signed "A.D.," shown in 1975 catalog, Code #55. The same code number was assigned to *Ole King Cole* in the 1965 catalog. $28.00-32.00

Sheriff Bear salt and pepper, range size, unmarked $15.00-18.00

Cookie Safe, mark very faint, but can see "copyright " and " '58," not listed in either catalog $28.00-32.00

Raccoon, "Twin Winton, copyright, Calif. USA" 1965 catalog, TW 92 $35.00-40.00

ROW 3: *Child in Shoe,* "Twin Winton, copyright Calif. USA" 1965 catalog, TW 82 $30.00-35.00

Cookie Shack, unmarked. 1965 catalog, TW 97 $28.00-32.00

Tepee, "Twin Winton, copyright Calif. USA" $65.00-70.00

Occasionally a Twin Winton jar will be found with the date of manufacture, such as *Dobbin* and the *Cookie Safe.*

LAMBS ONLY
P
S

POLICE
Cookie Safe

COOKIE CHIEF

ROW 1: *Friar Tuck,* 1965 catalog, TW 85, stamped: "Twin Winton, San Juan Capistrano, Calif. USA" $30.00-35.00

Friar Tuck salt and pepper, marked: "Twin Winton, copyright, Calif. USA" $15.00-18.00

Cookie Time Clock, 1965 catalog, TW 81 $28.00-32.00

Friar Tuck. This high-gloss version is missing the label, but you can see where it was. $30.00-35.00

ROW 2: *Cop,* 1965 catalog, TW 49, "Twin Winton, Calif. USA," both stamped and incised, artist initialed "J.M." The cop is also available in the Collectors' Series. $50.00-60.00

Hotei, 1965 catalog, TW 78, stamped: "Twin Winton, copyright, Calif. USA," artist signed "Em." $45.00-50.00

Butler, 1965 catalog, TW 60, "Twin Winton, copyright, Calif. USA" $50.00-60.00

ROW 3: *Ranger Bear* napkin holder, unmarked $18.00-22.00

Cows salt and pepper, range-size, unmarked $15.00-18.00

Kangaroo salt and pepper, range-size, marked: "Twin Winton, Calif. USA" $15.00-18.00

Cookie Shack, gold seal: "Beautiful Hand Crafted Ceramics, Made in USA, Twin Winton, San Juan Capistrano, Calif. 92675" $30.00-35.00

S
Thou shalt not steal!
P
COOKIE TIME
Thou shalt not steal!

ROW 1: *Coach,* stamped "Twin Winton San Juan Capistrano, Calif. USA" $55.00-65.00

Castle, "W copyright The Twin Wintons" $90.00-95.00

Jack in Box, salt and pepper range-size, "Twin Winton Calif. USA" $15.00-20.00

Jack in Box, "Twin Winton Calif. USA" $60.00-65.00

ROW 2: *Gun Fighter Rabbit,* stamped and engraved into pottery "Twin Winton Calif. USA," artist signed "Liz" $55.00-65.00

Duck with Drum, "Twin Wintons copyright Calif. USA" $45.00-50.00

Kangaroo, "Twin Winton Calif. USA" $45.00-50.00

ROW 3: *Donkey and Cart,* unmarked $60.00-65.00

Cookie Sack, "W copyright The Twin Wintons" $28.00-32.00

Fire Engine, "Twin Winton copyright Calif. USA" $40.00-45.00

BELOW: *Dog on Drum,* "Twin Winton copyright Calif. USA" $30.00-35.00

Poodle at Counter, "Twin Winton copyright Calif. USA" $35.00-38.00

Poodle salt and pepper, unmarked $15.00-20.00

Mother Goose, "Twin Winton, Made in Calif. USA copyright 1962" $30.00-35.00

GRANDMAS
COOK
FD

Walt Disney

Walter Elias Disney was born in Chicago, Illinois, on December 5, 1901. His career was launched in 1919 when he worked as a commercial artist and cartoonist; by 1928, Disney had produced his first successful sound picture, *Steamboat Willie.*

Walt Disney is an American tradition, synonymous with Mickey, Minnie, Donald, Alice, Cinderella, and many more.

Walt Disney signifies wholesome, family-oriented entertainment.

Through the years, many companies have been licensed for producing varied Disney products, including cookie jars. Earliest items may be copyrighted "Walt Disney Enterprises," while more current items are marked "Walt Disney Productions." Anything produced after 1984 will be marked "Walt Disney Company."

Though Walt Disney, the man, is gone, Walt Disney Productions continues and Disney collectibles are ever-growing.

ROW 1: *Single Joe Carioca,* "Joe Carioca from *The Three Caballeros.* Walt Disney USA," made by the Leeds China Company of Chicago, Illinois $125.00-150.00

Pinocchio, "Walt Disney, copyright, Productions, Cuernavaca, Mexico" $150.00-175.00

Pinocchio, "Copyright, Walt Disney Productions" $100.00-125.00

ROW 2: *Mary Poppins,* "Copyright, MCMLXIV, Walt Disney Productions" $80.00-90.00

Babes in Toyland, stamped: "Walt Disney Productions, copyright 1961." This jar was made by American Bisque for Disney. $70.00-80.00

Lollipop Jar, "Copyright, 1961 Walt Disney Productions" $50.00-60.00

ROW 3: *Professor Ludwig Von Drake,* "Copyright, Walt Disney USA 1961." Ludwig was made by American Bisque. $175.00-200.00

Mickey Mouse with music box in lid, Japan $70.00-80.00

Alice in Wonderland with looking-glass lid, unmarked $80.00-90.00

Mary Poppins
IT'S A JOLLY HOLIDAY
MICKEY MOUSE
MUSICAL MICKEY MOUSE
Alice in Wonder Land

ROW 1: *Pluto* side of *Dumbo/Pluto Turnabout,* "23 L copyright Walt Disney," made by the Leeds China Company of Chicago, Illinois $55.00-65.00

Dumbo side of *Dumbo/Pluto Turnabout,* marked as above $55.00-65.00

Standing Donald Duck, "copyright Walt Disney USA" $150.00-175.00

Donald Duck salt and pepper, unmarked $15.00-18.00

ROW 2: *Mickey Mouse* side of *Mickey/Minnie Turnabout,* "Patented Turnabout 4 in 1 Mickey and Minnie Walt Disney," a Leeds China product $50.00-60.00

Mickey, shaker by Leeds $12.00-15.00

Minnie Mouse side of *Mickey/Minnie Turnabout,* marked as above $50.00-60.00

Minnie, shaker by Leeds $12.00-15.00

Sitting Donald Duck, "Reg. U.S. Pat. Off. Celebrate Made in USA Walt Disney Productions," made by the American Bisque Company $80.00-90.00

Donald Duck, salt and pepper shaker, unmarked, also made by American Bisque $12.00-15.00

ROW 3: *Joe Carioca* side of *Donald Duck/Joe Carioca Turnabout,* "Donald Duck & Joe Carioca from *The Three Caballeros* Walt Disney USA," made by the Leeds China Company of Chicago, Illinois $55.00-65.00

Donald Duck side of *Donald Duck/Joe Carioca Turnabout,* marked as above $55.00-65.00

Single Joe Carioca, "Joe Carioca from *The Three Caballeros* copyright Walt Disney USA," made by The Leeds China, Chicago, Illinois. This single *Joe Carioca* has been found in two versions, cold painted and color applied underglaze. $125.00-150.00

The Leeds China Company was licensed to make Disney Characters from 1944 to 1954. The *Turnabouts* were produced in the late 1940's.

It is uncertain when American Bisque produced the *Sitting Donald Duck.* The Allen family has identified it as their product.

ROW 1:	*Eeyore,* "901 copyright Walt Disney Productions," made by California Originals	$100.00-115.00
	Winnie the Pooh, 900 Walt Disney Productions USA," made by California Originals	$75.00-85.00
	Tigger, "Walt Disney Productions 902," made by California Originals	$90.00-100.00
ROW 2:	*Birthday Cake,* produced for Mickey's 50th birthday, "Walt Disney Productions"	$90.00-100.00
	Mickey Mouse Car, "copyright Walt Disney Productions, copyright Sears, Roebuck and Co. 1978, Japan"	$85.00-95.00
	Mickey Clock, "Walt Disney Productions" on the clock face, and a paper label: "Enesco WDE-219"	$115.00-125.00
ROW 3:	*Dumbo Turnabout,* "Patented Turnabout 4 - 1 Dumbo copyright Walt Disney," made by the Leeds China Company, Chicago, Illinois in late 1940's.	$50.00-60.00
	Thumper, "Reg. U.S. Pat. Off. Celebrate, Made in USA"	$50.00-60.00
	Thumper, salt and pepper shakers, "copyright Walt Disney Productions"	$18.00-22.00
	Dumbo Turnabout, reverse side, marked as above	$50.00-60.00

COOKIES

HAPPY
BIRTHDAY
COOKIES
MICKEY MOUSE
COOKIE TIME

ROW 1: *Donald Duck* cylinder, made by California Originals $35.00-45.00

Mickey and Donald cookie tin, unmarked $30.00-35.00

Dumbo cylinder, made by California Originals $35.00-45.00

ROW 2: *Donald Duck and Pumpkin,* "Walt Disney Productions 805," made by California Originals $65.00-75.00

Dumbo's Greatest Cookies on Earth, "copyright Walt Disney Prod. U.S.A. 969," made by California Originals $60.00-70.00

Mickey Mouse and Drum, "Walt Disney Productions #864," made by California Originals $75.00-85.00

ROW 3: *Winnie the Pooh,* "copyright, Sears, Roebuck, and Co. 1982, Made in Japan" $65.00-75.00

Mickey's 50th Anniversary tin, unmarked $35.00-45.00

Winnie the Pooh "Hunny Pot," "#907" inside lid, made by California Originals $70.00-80.00

BELOW: *Leather-ear Mickey,* "copyright Walt Disney Prod.," paper label: "Enesco." $60.00-70.00

Uncle Scrooge bank, "copyright Walt Disney Productions, Ceramica de Cvernavaca" $200.00-225.00

DUMBO'S
GREATEST COOKIES
ON
EARTH
Stauffer's
DISNEY
COOKIES
ALL NATURAL
NET WT. 7 OZ. (198.4g)

HAPPY BIRTHDAY
MICKEY
50 YEARS OF MAGIC
HUNNY

ROW 1:	*Mickey Mouse,* "copyright The Walt Disney Co. by HOAN Ltd."	$40.00-45.00
	Snow White, "Walt Disney Production," "Enesco" label	$100.00-110.00
	Donald Duck Head, "Walt Disney Productions WD5," label: "Original Dan Brechner Exclusive, Japan"	$100.00-110.00
	Donald Duck, "copyright Walt Disney Co. by HOAN Ltd."	$40.00-45.00
ROW 2:	*Big Al,* "Walt Disney Productions," made by Treasure Craft	$60.00-70.00
	Ring Master, "Gepetto Pottery from Walt Disney Pinocchio, Trademark Reg. U.S. Pat. Office," a Brayton Laguna Production	$200.00-225.00
	Pinocchio, "Calif. Orig. G-131 U.S.A."	$125.00-150.00
ROW 3:	*Goofy's Cookie Co.,* "copyright Walt Disney Productions 862, USA," made by California Originals	$125.00-150.00
	Pinocchio with Fish Bowl, "copyright Walt Disney Productions 867 USA," made by California Originals	$150.00-160.00
	Bambi, "copyright Walt Disney Prod. USA 868," also made by California Originals	$80.00-90.00

FLOUR
DONALD DUCK
COOKIES
GOOFYS
COOKIE CO

Bibliography

Davern, Melva, *The Collector's Encyclopedia of Salt and Pepper Shakers, Figural and Novelty.* Collector Books, Paducah, Kentucky.

Derwich, Jenny B. and Latos, Dr. Mary, *Dictionary Guide to United States Pottery & Porcelain* (19th and 20th Century). Jenstan, Research in United States Pottery and Porcelain, P.O. Box 674, Franklin, Michigan 48025.

Huxford, Sharon and Bob, *The Collector's Encyclopedia of Brush McCoy Pottery;* Collector Books, Paducah, Kentucky.

Huxford, Sharon and Bob, *The Collector's Encyclopedia of McCoy Pottery.* Collector Books, Paducah, Kentucky.

Lehner, Lois, *Lehner's Encyclopedia of U.S. Marks on Pottery, Porcelain, & Clay.* Collector Books, Paducah, Kentucky.

Nichols, Harold, *McCoy Cookie Jars, From the First to the Latest.* Nichols Publishing, Ames, Iowa.

Simon, Dolores, *Red Wing Pottery with Rumrill.* Collector Books, Paducah, Kentucky.

Newsletters

Curran, Pam, Shawnee Pottery Collector's Club, P.O. Box 713, New Smyrna Beach, Florida 32170-0713

Davern, Melva, Novelty Salt and Pepper Shakers Club, P.O. Box 81914, Pittsburgh, Pennsylvania 15217

Dole, Pat, *The New Glaze,* P.O. Box 782, Birmingham, Alabama 35206

Greenwood, Jacquie, *The Black Memorabilia Collector's Monthly Newsletter,* no longer available.

Lynch, Kathy, *Our McCoy Matters,* 12704 Lockleven,Woolbridge, Virginia 22192.

Roerig, Joyce, *Cookie Jarrin' with Joyce: THE Cookie Jar Newsletter,* Route 2, Box 504, Walterboro, South Carolina 29488

Catalogs

Winton, Twin, *A Catalog of the Nation's Best-Selling Cookie Jars in Wood Finish and The Nostalgic.* Special editions for 1965 and 1975.

Index

Books on Antiques and Collectibles

Most of the following books are available from your local book seller or antique dealer, or on loan from your public library. If you are unable to locate certain titles in your area you may order by mail from COLLECTOR BOOKS, P.O. Box 3009, Paducah, KY 42002-3009. Add $2.00 for postage for the first book ordered and $.25 for each additional book. Include item number, title and price when ordering. Allow 14 to 21 days for delivery. All books are well illustrated and contain current values.

Books on Glass and Pottery

1810 American Art Glass, Shuman $29.95
1517 American Belleek, Gaston $19.95
2016 Bedroom & Bathroom Glassware of the Depression Years $19.95
1312 Blue & White Stoneware, McNerney $9.95
1959 Blue Willow, 2nd Ed., Gaston $14.95
1627 Children's Glass Dishes, China & Furniture II, Lechler $19.95
1892 Collecting Royal Haeger, Garmon $19.95
1373 Collector's Ency of American Dinnerware, Cunningham $24.95
2133 Collector's Ency. of Cookie Jars, Roerig $24.95
2017 Collector's Ency. of Depression Glass, Florence, 9th Ed. $19.95
1812 Collector's Ency. of Fiesta, Huxford $19.95
1439 Collector's Ency. of Flow Blue China, Gaston $19.95
1961 Collector's Ency. of Fry Glass, Fry Glass Society $24.95
2086 Collector's Ency. of Gaudy Dutch & Welsh, Schuman $14.95
1813 Collector's Ency. of Geisha Girl Porcelain, Litts $19.95
1915 Collector's Ency. of Hall China, 2nd Ed., Whitmyer $19.95
1358 Collector's Ency. of McCoy Pottery, Huxford $19.95
1039 Collector's Ency. of Nippon Porcelain I, Van Patten $19.95
1350 Collector's Ency. of Nippon Porcelain II, Van Patten $19.95
1665 Collector's Ency. of Nippon Porcelain III, Van Patten $24.95
1447 Collector's Ency. of Noritake, Van Patten $19.95
1037 Collector's Ency. of Occupied Japan I, Florence $14.95
1038 Collector's Ency. of Occupied Japan II, Florence $14.95
1719 Collector's Ency. of Occupied Japan III, Florence $14.95
2019 Collector's Ency. of Occupied Japan IV, Florence $14.95
1715 Collector's Ency. of R.S. Prussia II, Gaston $24.95
1034 Collector's Ency. of Roseville Pottery, Huxford $19.95
1035 Collector's Ency. of Roseville Pottery, 2nd Ed., Huxford $19.95
1623 Coll. Guide to Country Stoneware & Pottery, Raycraft $9.95
2077 Coll. Guide Country Stone. & Pottery, 2nd Ed., Raycraft $14.95
1523 Colors in Cambridge, National Cambridge Society $19.95
1425 Cookie Jars, Westfall $9.95
1843 Covered Animal Dishes, Grist $14.95
1844 Elegant Glassware of the Depression Era, 4th Ed., Florence $19.95
2024 Kitchen Glassware of the Depression Years, 4th Ed., Florence $19.95
1465 Haviland Collectibles & Art Objects, Gaston $19.95
1917 Head Vases Id & Value Guide, Cole $14.95
1392 Majolica Pottery, Katz-Marks $9.95
1669 Majolica Pottery, 2nd Series, Katz-Marks $9.95
1919 Pocket Guide to Depression Glass, 7th Ed., Florence $9.95
1438 Oil Lamps II, Thuro $19.95
1670 Red Wing Collectibles, DePasquale $9.95
1440 Red Wing Stoneware, DePasquale $9.95
1958 So. Potteries Blue Ridge Dinnerware, 3rd Ed., Newbound $14.95
1889 Standard Carnival Glass, 2nd Ed., Edwards $24.95
1814 Wave Crest, Glass of C.F. Monroe, Cohen $29.95
1848 Very Rare Glassware of the Depression Years, Florence $24.95
2140 Very Rare Glassware of the Depression Years, Second Series $24.95

Books on Dolls & Toys

1887 American Rag Dolls, Patino $14.95
2079 Barbie Fashion, Vol. 1, 1959-1967, Eames $24.95
1749 Black Dolls, Gibbs $14.95
1514 Character Toys & Collectibles 1st Series, Longest $19.95
1750 Character Toys & Collectibles, 2nd Series, Longest $19.95
2021 Collectible Male Action Figures, Manos $14.95
1529 Collector's Ency. of Barbie Dolls, DeWein $19.95
1066 Collector's Ency. of Half Dolls, Marion $29.95
2151 Collector's Guide to Tootsietoys, Richter $14.95
2082 Collector's Guide to Magazine Paper Dolls, Young $14.95
1891 French Dolls in Color, 3rd Series, Smith $14.95
1631 German Dolls, Smith $9.95
1635 Horsman Dolls, Gibbs $19.95
1067 Madame Alexander Collector's Dolls, Smith $19.95
2025 Madame Alexander Price Guide #15, Smith $7.95
1995 Modern Collector's Dolls, Vol. I, Smith $19.95
1516 Modern Collector's Dolls Vol. V, Smith $19.95
1540 Modern Toys, 1930-1980, Baker $19.95
2033 Patricia Smith Doll Values, Antique to Modern, 6th Ed. $9.95
1886 Stern's Guide to Disney $14.95
2139 Stern's Guide to Disney, 2nd Series $14.95
1513 Teddy Bears & Steiff Animals, Mandel $9.95
1817 Teddy Bears & Steiff Animals, 2nd, Mandel $19.95
2084 Teddy Bears, Annalees & Steiff Animals, 3rd, Mandel $19.95
2028 Toys, Antique & Collectible, Longest $14.95
1648 World of Alexander-Kins, Smith $19.95
1808 Wonder of Barbie, Manos $9.95
1430 World of Barbie Dolls, Manos $9.95

Other Collectibles

1457 American Oak Furniture, McNerney $9.95
1846 Antique & Collectible Marbles, Grist, 2nd Ed. $9.95
1712 Antique & Collectible Thimbles, Mathis $19.95
1880 Antique Iron, McNerney $9.95
1748 Antique Purses, Holiner $19.95
1868 Antique Tools, Our American Heritage, McNerney $9.95
2015 Archaic Indian Points & Knives, Edler $14.95
1426 Arrowheads & Projectile Points, Hothem $7.95
1278 Art Nouveau & Art Deco Jewelry, Baker $9.95
1714 Black Collectibles, Gibbs $19.95
1666 Book of Country, Raycraft $19.95
1960 Book of Country Vol II, Raycraft $19.95
1811 Book of Moxie, Potter $29.95
1128 Bottle Pricing Guide, 3rd Ed., Cleveland $7.95
1751 Christmas Collectibles, Whitmyer $19.95
1752 Christmas Ornaments, Johnston $19.95
1713 Collecting Barber Bottles, Holiner $24.95
2132 Collector's Ency. of American Furniture, Vol. I, Swedberg $24.95
2018 Collector's Ency. of Graniteware, Greguire $24.95
2083 Collector's Ency. of Russel Wright Designs, Kerr $19.95
1634 Coll. Ency. of Salt & Pepper Shakers, Davern $19.95
2020 Collector's Ency. of Salt & Pepper Shakers II, Davern $19.95
2134 Collector's Guide to Antique Radios, Bunis $16.95
1916 Collector's Guide to Art Deco, Gaston $14.95
1753 Collector's Guide to Baseball Memorabilia, Raycraft $14.95
1537 Collector's Guide to Country Baskets, Raycraft $9.95
1437 Collector's Guide to Country Furniture, Raycraft $9.95
1842 Collector's Guide to Country Furniture II, Raycraft $14.95
1962 Collector's Guide to Decoys, Huxford $14.95
1441 Collector's Guide to Post Cards, Wood $9.95
1716 Fifty Years of Fashion Jewelry, Baker $19.95
2022 Flea Market Trader, 6th Ed., Huxford $9.95
1668 Flint Blades & Proj. Points of the No. Am. Indian, Tully $24.95
1755 Furniture of the Depression Era, Swedberg $19.95
2081 Guide to Collecting Cookbooks, Allen $14.95
1424 Hatpins & Hatpin Holders, Baker $9.95
1964 Indian Axes & Related Stone Artifacts, Hothem $14.95
2023 Keen Kutter Collectibles, 2nd Ed., Heuring $14.95
1181 100 Years of Collectible Jewelry, Baker $9.95
2137 Modern Guns, Identification & Value Guide, Quertermous $12.95
1965 Pine Furniture, Our Am. Heritage, McNerney $14.95
2080 Price Guide to Cookbooks & Recipe Leaflets, Dickinson $9.95
1124 Primitives, Our American Heritage, McNerney $8.95
1759 Primitives, Our American Heritage, 2nd Series, McNerney $14.95
2026 Railroad Collectibles, 4th Ed., Baker $14.95
1632 Salt & Pepper Shakers, Guarnaccia $9.95
1888 Salt & Pepper Shakers II, Guarnaccia $14.95
2141 Schroeder's Antiques Price Guide, 9th Ed. $12.95
2096 Silverplated Flatware, 4th Ed., Hagan $14.95
2027 Standard Baseball Card Pr. Gd., Florence $9.95
1922 Standard Bottle Pr. Gd., Sellari $14.95
1966 Standard Fine Art Value Guide, Huxford $29.95
2085 Standard Fine Art Value Guide Vol. 2, Huxford $29.95
2078 The Old Book Value Guide, 2nd Ed $19.95
1923 Wanted to Buy $9.95
1885 Victorian Furniture, McNerney $9.95

Schroeder's Antiques Price Guide

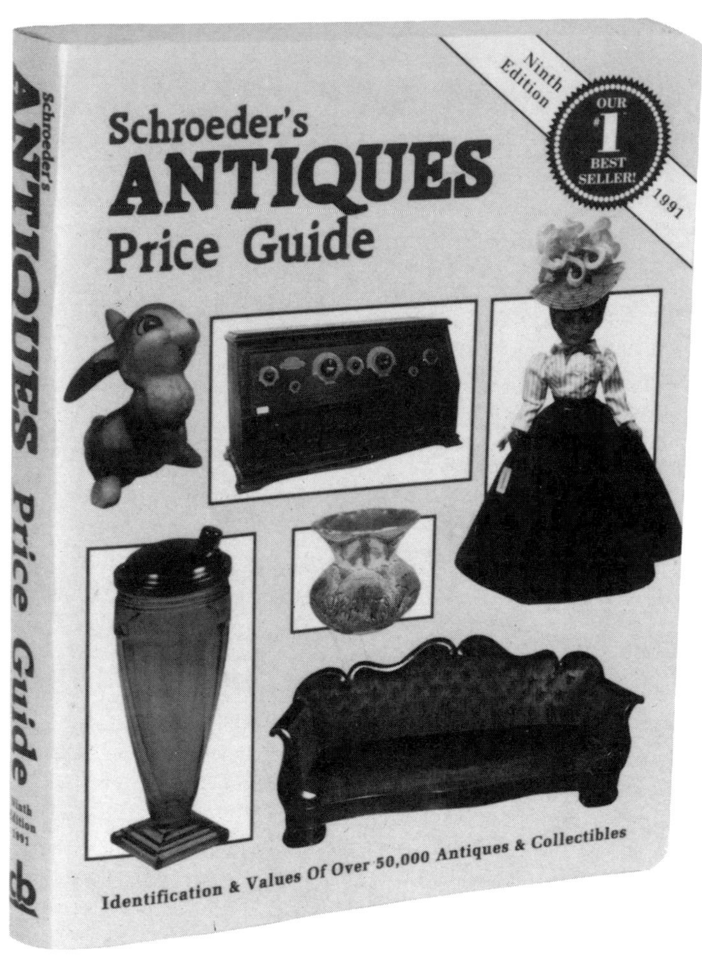

Schroeder's Antiques Price Guide has climbed its way to the top in a field already supplied with several well-established publications! The word is out, *Schroeder's Price Guide* is the best buy at any price. Over 500 categories are covered, with more than 50,000 listings. But it's not volume alone that makes Schroeder's the unique guide it is recognized to be. From ABC Plates to Zsolnay, if it merits the interest of today's collector, you'll find it in Schroeder's. Each subject is represented with histories and background information. In addition, hundreds of sharp original photos are used each year to illustrate not only the rare and the unusual, but the everyday "fun-type" collectibles as well -- not postage stamp pictures, but large close-up shots that show important details clearly.

Each edition is completely re-typeset from all new sources. We have not and will not simply change prices in each new edition. All new copy and all new illustrations make Schroeder's THE price guide on antiques and collectibles.

The writing and researching team behind this giant is proportionately large. It is backed by a staff of more than seventy of Collector Books' finest authors, as well as a board of advisors made up of well-known antique authorities and the country's top dealers, all specialists in their fields. Accuracy is their primary aim. Prices are gathered over the entire year previous to publication, from ads and personal contacts. Then each category is thoroughly checked to spot inconsistencies, listings that may not be entirely reflective of actual market dealings, and lines too vague to be of merit. Only the best of the lot remains for publication. You'll find *Schroeder's Antiques Price Guide* the one to buy for factual information and quality.

No dealer, collector or investor can afford not to own this book. It is available from your favorite bookseller or antiques dealer at the low price of $12.95. If you are unable to find this price guide in your area, it's available from Collector Books, P. O. Box 3009, Paducah, KY 42001 at $12.95 plus $2.00 for postage and handling.

8½ x 11, 608 Pages $12.95

COLLECTOR BOOKS

A Division of Schroeder Publishing Co., Inc.